THE BEST CANADIAN POETRY IN ENGLISH 2008

The Best
Canadian Poetry
in English

2008

Edited by
Stephanie Bolster

Series Editor
Molly Peacock

Tightrope Books

Tightrope Books
17 Greyton Crescent
Toronto, Ontario
Canada M6E 2G1
www.tightropebooks.com

EDITOR: Stephanie Bolster
SERIES EDITOR: Molly Peacock
MANAGING EDITOR: Heather Wood
COPY EDITOR: Shirarose Wilensky
COVER DESIGN: David Bigham
TYPESETTING: Carleton Wilson

Produced with the support of the Canada Council for the Arts, the Ontario Arts Council and the City of Toronto through the Toronto Arts Council.

Printed in Canada

LIBRARY AND ARCHIVES CANADA CATALOGUING IN PUBLICATION

The best Canadian poetry in English, 2008 : yearly anthology /
edited by Stephanie Bolster.

ISBN 978-0-9783351-7-5

1. Canadian poetry (English)–21st century. I. Bolster, Stephanie

PS8293.1.B48 2008   c811'.608   C2008-904882-2

CONTENTS

Welcome to *The Best Canadian Poetry in English 2008*, the first anthology of its kind in Canada, and the inaugural volume of a yearly series that hopes to collect the freshest, the brightest, the most exciting, compelling and vigorous poems published in Canada's literary journals from the previous year.

Canadian English language poetry is a dynamic art, and those literary journals that publish poetry reshape the landscape of Canadian letters every year. Yet few of us, even the most avid poetry-trackers, peruse all these magazines, and many of us are bewildered by their abundance. This is the primary reason for our yearly series. Our annual pulse-taking will track the birth of ideas, language, and rhythms of culture across the English Canadian poetic landscape. As well, it will highlight the emergence of new voices and the renaissance of familiar voices. From sound poems to confessional poems, from loose-limbed narratives to formal verse, from bellows to whispers, from the avenues to the bush, from west to east and all directions in between, prosodic decisions, geographical propensities and cultural proclivities give Canadian poetry its astonishing variety. *The Best Canadian Poetry in English* addresses both the confusion and the plethora by narrowing the field, providing a kind of qualifying finals for poetry every year.

Literary magazines are often the first places a poet publishes, usually long before a poet collects the work into book form. For this reason, editors of literary magazines stand as discoverers and take on the role of literary explorers, searching out and discovering the vibrant and the new among poets.

For *The Best Canadian Poetry in English* series we review as many issues of literary journals from the previous year as possible. Because we do not believe that a committee, with all its compromises, can select the best poems, each year we will pick a single poet-editor to choose among the chosen for our volume. Although I will remain as the series editor, the guest poet-editor will change annually. We hope by these changes to reflect the aesthetic vigour and the wild diversity in inclination and taste among Canadian poets – or maybe I should say among Canadian poetries.

Our inaugural poet-editor is Stephanie Bolster, a Governor General's Award-winning Montreal poet who has published three volumes of poetry, and who has undertaken with the support of Tightrope Books Editor and Publisher Halli Villegas and myself, to beat the ground for literary magazines, to read voraciously, all the poetry published in English this year, and to choose, with courage and trepidation, the fifty poems that comprise this first volume and the list of fifty more of note. Her record of her adventures follows in the Introduction, and we thank her for the hard work she undertook in her trailblazing effort.

Stephanie Bolster[1] is exclusively responsible for selecting these spicy, contemplative dynamos. Because of her eclectic taste and her formidable sense of what comprises excellence, the poems range in tone from the reverent (two meditative poems, Maleea Acker's "The Reflecting Pool" and Leif E. Vaage's "Shrove Tuesday," open and close the book) to the word-besotted (Margaret Avison's "Hag-Ridden" and "There, there" by Sadiqua de Meijer come to mind); and range in subject from taxidermy – yes, you read that right – in Aurian Haller's long poem "Song of the Taxidermist," to the contemplation of a coverlet made suspiciously of "100% UNDETERMINED FIBERS" in Craig Poile's lyric poem "The Blanket." Nature is everywhere, from Yvonne Blomer's "The Roll Call to the Ark" to Don McKay's "Sleeping with the River" and that special brand of nature-based Canadian surrealism practised by Jason Heroux in "Lost Forest." Many of these poets seem to pay homage to their influences, from Helen Humphreys' "Auden's House" and Tim Lilburn's "Orphic Hymn" to Michael Lista's

1. I never communicated with Bolster about her choices during the decision-making process, in part because I am the poetry editor of the *Literary Review of Canada*, which submits poems to be considered for *The Best Canadian Poetry in English*, but also because I know when I am shouldering the responsibility for judging, I prefer to be left alone. In the interests of full disclosure I should mention that Bolster selected poems that the LRC published, as well as a poem that won the CBC Literary Award for 2007, which I helped to judge.

"The Scale of Intensity," after a poem by Don Paterson, and Leanne Averbach's reckoning with Virginia Woolf, "To the Lighthouse." These poems tend towards the virtuoso performance as well, giving ample evidence of Canadian formalism – yes, the Canadian sonnet does exist, and we have one here, "Spineless Sonnet" by Jason Guriel. There is also a whole sonnet sequence by John Barton called "One Bedroom Apartment." The choices span the dense and the sumptuous, such as Barry Dempster's "Blindness;" the fearlessly emotional, Susan Elmslie's "Box," for instance; and the sharply imagistic, such as Anne Compton's "Stars, Sunday Dawn," or Jeramy Dodds' noun-studded "The Gift."

There are long, take-your-time poems, like Méira Cook's jaunty "A Walker in the City," Keith Maillard's "July," and E. Alex Pierce's "To float, to drown, to close up, to open – a throat," as well as shorter lyrical poems that depend on touchstone visual images almost as paintings do. A. F. Moritz demonstrates this impulse in his poem, "Odds and Ends," and so does Jim Nason in "Chardin's Rabbit," which suggests in its very title how poetry is tied to painting. Heather Sellers drives the Florida landscape into a painterly three-stanza portrait of the contemporary family in "I Don't Remember Telling the Stepsons."

The idea of collecting the best poetry of the past year is a distinctly American idea, the brainchild of the poet David Lehman, which has now spread to other countries, like an American export brand. As it turns out, our first volume of *The Best Canadian Poetry in English* is as different from its US counterpart as Canadian poetry itself differs from what is written to the south.

But what is it, exactly, this best Canadian poem in English for this year? It seems to me that it is a poem that takes its time, but does not lose its intensity. One that wanders but is not afraid of getting lost; a poem that is willing to stumble because it takes on rough or unknown emotional or intellectual terrain, but rights itself again; a poem that admits a reader as a companion, a worthy witness to experience, whether that experience is a heady, brainy one, or a quiet, domestic few minutes. That the poems for this year proceed in time without losing intensity means that each one is forged of passion and heated with a virtuosity of craft. I would say that passion and virtuosity are exactly the characteristics of the best Canadian poetry of 2008 in English.

If you've read this far – and I don't really expect you to, because if you're holding this anthology, you're probably thumbing through the poems themselves – you'll notice that I have not spoken about Canada's cultural multiplicity, though it is in ample representation here. What I see, from poets from diverse backgrounds, provinces, ages and personal categories, is a unity, a core, something identifiable as a gesture in Canadian poetry itself, not in the poets' backgrounds or personalities, but in the poems they produce, poems that presume a kind of companionship with their readers and assume their readers' willingness to undertake a tandem adventure. They are not poems that stand apart from an audience, inviting the audience to watch them, and in this they are distinct from many of their American and British counterparts. Instead, these poems often fully enter the imaginative ground where writer and reader are one.

Think of this volume as a swimming pool. Poet and reader go in together. Finally they hit the place where their feet leave the bottom, and then they swim, experiencing something they both know is over their heads. That is what poetry is: trying to stay afloat in an element in which you might sink, and which is surely over your head. This is what makes *The Best Canadian Poetry in English 2008* as exhilarating as it is, this, and the paradox that it presents, for what is a mere year to the art that is supposed to be timeless? These poems tell us that even the timeless begins somewhere.

Molly Peacock
TORONTO

Who do you think you are? The phrase, inseparable in the minds of Canadian readers from Alice Munro's book of that title, has arisen in a number of discussions with fellow writers over the years, refer- ring specifically to the reluctance – in these conversations posited as particularly Canadian and, though perhaps secondarily, particularly female – to pronounce a viewpoint. It appeared in a thought bubble over my head when I received an e-mail from Halli Villegas early in 2007, asking if I would edit the first annual *The Best Canadian Poetry in English.* The invitation came as a surprise, an honour, and a privilege, one that I hesitated to accept not because of the inevitable time-drain but because of the responsibility.

Though a reader of the *Best American* annuals, I've always balked at "best." I don't have the same "best" from year to year, perhaps not even from morning to night within a single day. And yet the notion of quality is implicit in so much of a poet's work; we submit only those poems that we think are the best, the editors of journals publish those that they think are the best, and so on.

No escaping the evaluative, then. A Canadian anthology of this kind was long overdue, someone would have to edit it, and following the single-editor model of the American series would avoid lowest-com- mon-denominator choices. As an active writer, reader, and teacher of Canadian poetry – who had a sabbatical coming up – I was, I decided, ready to accept the task.

Rules were set, some by Halli, some by Molly Peacock, some by me, some by the triumvirate: one hundred poems, of which the top fifty would be included in the anthology. No more than one poem per poet. No to poems by Canadian poets published in American journals (they fell into the domain of *Best American*). No to poems by American and other international writers published in Canadian journals (they risked going against Canada Council funding regulations). No to translations, unless they departed from the original sufficiently to be considered new work. Yes to long poems. No to including more than one poem from a series; excerpts from such series were permissible, but only if they stood alone. No to previously published work. The reading material was every 2007-dated issue of every literary journal published in Canada, excluding online and student publications.[1]

Most weeks, at least one journal thunked onto the vestibule floor. When the stack was too massive for our mail slot, the postwoman rang the doorbell, a hefty handful of publications in her hands and a slight crease between her eyebrows: was this bounty gift or punishment? Both, I'll confess, alternately and simultaneously.

In the classes I teach, we discuss what makes a poem and, then, what makes a good poem. Faced with a table-full of (for the most part supposedly nonconformist) students looking for clear and easy answers – what do I have to do to get an A? to get published? – I feel markedly unauthoritative. My list of criteria includes such categories as craft, communication, imagination, impact, and cohesiveness, with sub-elements ranging from *duende* to that troublesome pair, clarity and ambiguity.

As I read 2007's possible contenders – each on several occasions, to increase a poem's chances of striking me in a receptive moment – what was I looking for? First: good writing. Awkward or rote syntax; familiar expressions, images, and locutions; or random lineation, ruled a poem out. A meaningfully rebellious and distinctive syntax or a deliberately dissonant music often ruled it in. Second: depth and challenge, be that emotional or intellectual. If additional readings failed to yield new insights and appreciations, but rather, dulled the flash I'd sensed the first time around, the poem lost its Post-it note. Finally, and inseparable from the first two criteria: an interesting, even strange, sensibility or imagination. (As an undergrad, I fumed when one of my instructors remarked that my poems failed to startle. I didn't want to startle; surely the startle factor was overrated. Only later did I realize that what I did want to do – to please – doomed my poems to mediocrity.) "Startling"

1. The only exception would prove to be *Arc* #59, which appeared in 2007 and would have been dated Winter 2007 had a change in the journal's dating format not made it Winter 2008. I considered it anyway, in part because *Arc*'s only other 2007 issue consisted of republished work.

need not imply clatter and flash. I sought poems that excited and surprised me, that felt (boldly or quietly) necessary, often urgent. I sought poems serious and poems frivolous (though seriously frivolous). Those poems that played it safe, that failed to follow through on the risks they initiated, or that took risks apparently for their own sake, without integrity of form and content, did not make it into the anthology, though some distinguished themselves enough to appear on the long list. I was without doubt a tougher critic than if I'd been reading fewer poems, but asking myself whether I could confidently put my name behind a particular choice forced me to be discerning.

As a writer interested in process and in the cumulative, and as someone whose own poems tend to shine more brightly when surrounded by my other poems in a book than when surrounded by other poets' poems in a journal, I found this concentration on product and on the singular disconcerting. It troubled me that a poem that was, within the lifetime output of Writer X, mediocre, might be a standout when considered against the other poems in the issue in which it appeared and in 2007 generally. But reputations could not matter; this is and must be a collection not of poets but of poems.

Before I began the selection process, I believed that the range of work being written in this country was not reflected in our journals. I now believe that it is, though not in any single issue or journal. Editorial boards have, against their best intentions, a consensus-driven, streamlining effect.[2] This anthology, in distilling the year's output, showcases a greater range of work than any of the journals in which the poems originally appeared.

2. That said, despite my professed unease with the mainstream, two of the country's most visible literary journals, *The Malahat Review* and *The Fiddlehead*, garnered the most inclusions. Somewhat surprising, too (to me, at least, given that I'm often disappointed in contest winners) is the fact that a number of these poems already came highly recommended, having won national writing contests. (The two that went on to win National Magazine Awards – Aurian Haller's "Song of the Taxidermist" and Anne Compton's "Stars, Sunday Dawn" – did so long after I had selected them.) I am disappointed that

Prior to 2007, I suspected that there were too many literary journals. I now feel that the greater problem is that many journals are too voluminous.[3] I hoped not to have to say this. I've subscribed to literary journals for nearly two decades but have – like most subscribers, I suspect – rarely read them in their entirety. My Great Binge of 2007, though never regrettable, confirmed that scanning and skipping are not entirely misguided strategies. This is not to say that I wouldn't have missed some excellent poems had I followed my usual practice of perusing the Contents page and bio notes for familiar names and intriguing titles, then scanning the journal itself for compelling first lines or forms. But at times the process felt, though not exactly like looking for a needle in a haystack (as Billy Collins suggests in his Introduction to *The Best American Poetry 2006*, p. xv), not unlike panning for gold in the Yukon circa 1897. Flecks and nuggets appeared with sufficient regularity for me to go back to my tent every night rather than packing up and hitting the road, but, at times, weeks went by without that gleam in my pan.

I found very little bad writing. Instead, I read a great deal of competent poetry, most of it in the first-person lyric mode. It was, at times, death (despair, frustration, anger, stupor) by a hundred windows, rivers, aches/hearts/kitchen sinks. I've written about these things, too,

there is not work in this book from all of the journals I read – for each presented poems that I marked with Post-it notes, folded corners, and asterisks – but my decision to prioritize poems over poets or journals meant that if Poet Y presented several strong poems in various journals, I chose the one I thought most compelling, regardless of where it appeared. Some journals whose names do not appear here (*Filling Station* and PRECIPICe, for example) published fine work by writers whose names do appear. Other such journals included excellent poems by writers who turned out not to be Canadian. Yet this disappointment over journal representation was offset by my pleasure that *Border Crossings*, which is less well known for its poetry than for its visual art, was included, as were *Vallum* and *QWERTY*, two younger journals that, if I'm not mistaken, have primarily regional reputations in Canada.

3. A variation of this sentiment, made with respect to individually authored poetry books, was voiced by Robyn Sarah in "In Praise of Smaller Servings: On Publishing Poetry."(*Little Eurekas*. Emeryville, Ontario: Biblioasis, 2007. pp. 37–43.)

and often. I know, from experience, how important it is to find acceptance of one's work, especially early in one's career. I recognize that journals have commitments to subscribers and funding bodies, that prevent editors from simply deciding not to publish in a given season or to whittle an issue down to a flyer's scantness. (Six decades ago, George Dillon and Hayden Carruth, then editors of *Poetry*, incurred wrath when, due to a perceived lack of quality submissions, they published an issue containing 11 pages of its eponymous matter.) But I'm increasingly sympathetic to *Poetry*'s current editor Christian Wiman's remarks that "the more respect you have for poetry, the less of it you will find adequate to your taste and needs." While I don't believe, as he does, that "there is no such thing as a perfectly adequate poem, because a poem into which some strange and surprising excellence has not entered, a poem that is not in some inexplicable way beyond the will of the poet, is not a poem,"[4] I do believe that without such excellence, the poem is not a good one. While every poem that is written deserves to have been written, every poem that is published does not merit publication.

A disappointment in this process has been recognizing how few of this country's established writers publish in journals. Reading these journals made me feel nostalgic, which is to say old. It seems that those who seek publication, and presumably those who read journals, most avidly are those beginning their publishing careers. Perhaps it's simply that the editors – like me, looking for something new – turn away work by writers whose reputations and styles are already known to them. Or perhaps it's as John Barton wrote in "Where Have All the Poets Gone,"[5] established writers don't send their work out – being either too busy, too lazy, or too fearful of rejection – and emerging writers have found other forums, most notably online. American journals regularly solicit work from established writers and it may be time for more Canadian journals to begin this practice. It was a pleasure to find poems by P.K.

4. "In Praise of Rareness," *Poetry*, Vol. 189, No 3, December 2006

5. *Books in Canada*, Vol. 36, No. 3, April 2007, pp. 31–32.

Page, Don McKay, Lorna Crozier, Margaret Atwood, Al Moritz, Barry Dempster, and one precious poem by the late Margaret Avison. But where are Roo Borson, Don Coles, Anne Carson, Jan Zwicky, Don Domanski, Dionne Brand, and Erin Mouré? Surely they are not all in the midst of fallow periods – or, conversely, periods in which they're so productive that they're too busy to submit? Are they submitting work internationally instead? Going straight to book publication? Surely publishing in journals is, and should remain, essential to any writer wishing to be part of the country's poetic conversation?

Yet, all told, the pleasures of guest editing have far exceeded the disappointments and discouragement. A chief pleasure has been discovering (in a Columbus sense, for someone else was already there first) excellent poems by writers whose names were previously unknown to me, among them Jason Guriel and Michael Lista, each of whom presented several fine candidates.

Comments on the nature of the poems included here are best made by someone other than the person who selected them. Doubtless, my own aesthetic, which I've come to think of as alt.lyric, is reflected, though I endeavoured, as I do in the classroom, to read each poem on its own terms. Part of what convinced me to edit this year's anthology was the knowledge that another poet would take on the task next year; other approaches will bring other "bests," themselves also reflective of evolutions in Canadian poetry. If being the first guest editor has been a daunting responsibility, it's also spared me concerns about repeating or varying the aesthetic and poets of previous editions.

Based on only a year's thorough reading of the journals, it's difficult and unwise to make any bold, broad statements about trends; unlike fashion, in which the announcement of a trend brings the trend into being, poetry trends are best assessed in retrospect. That said, I offer some observations. Quirky, wacky, noisy, dense, disjunctive poems seem to be on the increase, perhaps through an influence of work from south of the border (see Ken Babstock's "Hunter Deary and Hospital Wing," Jeramy Dodds' "The Gift," Kevin Connolly's "Last One on the Moon," Méira Cook's "A Walker in the City," and Matt Rader's

"The Great Leap Forward"). So do their more subdued variants: oneiric, atmospheric poems such as Shane Rhodes' "If it was the sea we heard," John Wall Barger's "Weather," and Jason Heroux's "Lost Forest." 2007 saw the publication of some deft interpretations of form (Jason Guriel's "Spineless Sonnet," John Barton's sonnet corona "One Bedroom Apartment," Keith Maillard's "July" ghazals) and some moving takes on the found poem (Leanne Averbach's "To the Lighthouse" and Brian Bartlett's "Dear Georgie"), as well as some very fine long poems (the aforementioned Méira Cook and Keith Maillard, and Jeffrey Donaldson's "Museum") – not surprising given Canada's history of excellence and experimentation in this sub-genre. Then there are the expected subjects: animals (Yvonne Blomer's "The Roll Call to the Ark," Barry Dempster's "Blindness," Aurian Haller's "Song of the Taxidermist," Iain Higgins' "A Digression on Hunting," Jim Nason's "Chardin's Rabbit," David Seymour's "Song for the Call of the Richardson's Ground Squirrel...") and nature (Maleea Acker's "The Reflecting Pool," Don McKay's "Sleeping with the River," A.F. Moritz's "Odds and Ends," Michael Eden Reynolds' "A-frame," J.R. Toriseva's "Encyclopedia of Grass," Leif E. Vaage's "Shrove Tuesday"). Rather surprisingly, given the current state of national and world affairs, there is almost no overtly political work, though covert politics are everywhere.

What these poems share is a lively sense of the creative process. Each feels to me – and this after many readings – alive. Each – certainly the fifty printed here, but also many of the one hundred – brought something into my world that was not there before.

Though I still wonder who I think I am, I stand by these one hundred poems – which are themselves part of who I have been this past year, for they have followed me through my days, have inspired and baffled and moved me. And now, without further ado, I give them over to you, and you over to them.

Stephanie Bolster
MONTREAL

The Best Canadian Poetry in English 2008

The Reflecting Pool

Illuminated by early evening sun, we walked to where the pool lies,
into the yielding forest, which shrugged when we tried to praise.

Inside its amalgam of shadow and cessation, the glassy pond
aimed its whole self down to the centre of the earth.

There was another world inside. Taut against the stick
and moss disorder, the water inscribed edge without movement.

It loved so thoroughly the small branches of the overhanging fir,
the dead, spindled tumbles of emptied pine cones, the luminescence

of twinflower, wolf moss, fairy cup, mud. Its reaching became
an imitating eye, and the mirror elegy to what it loved.

Because it chose, we could see all things twice, and so had the chance
of glimpsing, the second time, what we always first ignore.

And as the water fell away, it took the image of the forest
and stretched it to the greenest shadows, taking our eyes

further and further down, and in. Its lofted breadth
ravelled the tapestry, learned every movement, armed gravity,

arraying knowledge in its rightness and its pull.

Americans

Your eyelashes: there's
what I know about Anacapri.
And spelling out time in flashes, a lighthouse.
And the bright houses drowning
down by the sea. We swam. We drank.
We passed a bottle on the waves in the dark.

In Pompeii, that was buried by fire,
we ate smoke from a living tongue.
Your skin, your skin. A cinder tree's shade;
a polyglot boy sold parasols,
and there were dogs alive and dead. A three-
legged mutt turning circles: no omen,
no omen we knew. In Assisi,

where broad and shallow steps crosscut
and veered from street to street,
we feared the holy orders. At Tivoli,
we leaned on a balustrade. At Frascati,
were cooled by a spigot.

Why does the tourist mind
always linger? It can't do a lick of good. But
you are my eyes' temple,
and I've adored you where you stood.

To the Lighthouse

I. THE WINDOW

The sun up to its lips in sky   Woolf lists waves   A frame shivering
lace   (Here she refers to a series of echoes)   The wide lawn veined
with tree   Our frail bark   And he stood by the urn as a point
on the terrace   The Lost Scholar   She thought (a common
illness See: S. Freud)   The strange equation marriage   Catenates
the mind   Never did anyone look so   Mothers, sons, a summer
house   Perfect empty tide   to the lighthouse

II. TIME PASSES

Now the question of the ten years   Her *Outline* reads: Dissolution,
gradual everything   The War   Women cleaning oblivion up
We are handed children   The devouring accumulates
Son "lost" in war   She slept life

III. THE LIGHTHOUSE

The living son steers to lighthouse with Father, "his scholar fence of
sanctity"   See *Moments of Being* pp. 40–41   (On shore watching
them, an attitude of easel)   Another sun up to its lips in blue
As after a long illness, bomb-vivid   Where the moment (threw out
like radium)   Very Woolf, this robe of flesh   (Artist thinks
from shore: Why create?   Canvas to end beneath sofa
And marriage, a slipper dangling from its famous foot)
The boat drowses in the bay   Father, son, sandwiches,
silence and so on   Then crinolines of sea
Wave-smashing light creasing rock   The beach, now
the lighthouse, its quick white shape   It was one's body
The flourishing centre   The already half out of the picture
She will later paint a trail "Intolerable"   (There is evidence
of condensing here)   Some gash in the lousy sea   Some bed
in the wood   Some essays, room, and so on

Hag-Ridden

A plague of locusts is
a reminder that the
focus on knees and thighs
in stringy and gangling
insects can inspire in-
vidious
comparisons.
Nimble in
chain-armour (below) with an
upsidedown carapace (shellacked),
these tiny
obstreperousnesses model
adoptable fashion trends.

The elderly, too,
are scant in under-
pinnings, and
angular. But,
unlike the locusts, these
swarm very seldom. Each may
go with a stick; a plague, perhaps first to
themselves. Yet, their
undemanding pleasure in the
world out under such a
mysterious (some days dazzling) sky
may be a tó-be-
desired infection.

Hunter Deary and Hospital Wing

Hunter Deary emits noises like peach pits;
  dry, scrotal humming that punctuates fits.
When a hip comes loose it comes loose
  before breakfast and she pops it back

in with a winch, a rock, a clean tube and a sock.
  Ask Hunter Deary what the microbes
are for. Ask Hunter Deary what the library's
  for. Ask Hunter Deary what agent con-

tested her birthright, her being out late, her
  transmission on broadband at night.
The men in the neon X. The hole in the
  plastic. The ppb. The stitches. The snug.

The snug. The stitches. The parts per billion.
        Hospital Wing sings to his children.
Children of blood lung.
Children of static.
        Hospital Wing sings to his children.
The snug. The stitches. The parts per billion.

Hunter Deary has clicked on the task pane
  reads there what they cut from the thought:
a topographical map of the region, a vein
  darkening wetlands, strung north through

some temperate zone. Hunter Deary left gas
  in a bird's nest, bags under bypasses,
phenobarbital in the mud of the Don. Hunter
  Deary in traction. Hunter Deary in Huntsville.

She's counting down days to a hearing; fed
  on black pumpkin, on cheese string, on
marrow sucked through wing of an auk. Ages
  in ice bubble. Calving. The fake vermillion.

Calving. The ages in bubbles. The fake vermillion.
    Hospital Wing sings to his children.
Children born sexless and cleansed.
Leaded gametes in frog ponds.
    Hospital Wing sings to his children.
Calving. The ages in bubbles. The fake vermillion.

Weather

Holding a spade in moonlight behind the café
where we ate lunch this afternoon.
Silver. Silver garbage cans and clotheslines and fences.
Air itself radioactive, cold.
                            What is there to dig for?
You are on a plane over the Atlantic.
Nothing tells me what to think of this.
So here I am gouging clean triangles of grass,
letting the spade claw through.

Amber in batterylight, café floorboards
above – umber, stone, anger,
  – and always, beyond the flat end of blade,
the object (is it *you?*) asphyxiating,
just out of time.
                   I strike metal –
a chill through the handle
and my arm sockets. A small tin box.
Unlocked. Inside, a book labelled *Weather*.
Sepia photos, corn fields spangled
with grit or UFOs. Veined stalks of funnel clouds, dust
devils, rainbows over splayed livestock,
page after page of signs, bad skies
drifting to sea.
                Chill morning light
from the cave mouth. No birds. This
on the first damp page:

You are gone, in a child's silver scrawl.

Dear Georgie

Extracted from letters written in October 1918 by Hermon Lawrence of Bayside, New Brunswick, to his older sister, my grandmother, Georgie Bartlett. She was then a 22-year-old with a year-old son; he was a 20-year-old enlisted in the Canadian Army and training – as he detailed at the end of each letter – in "the 3rd Heavy Canadian Battery, Composite Bridge, Witley Camp, Surrey, Eng." The Dwight mentioned below was their brother.

The war news have been good for quite awhile
but I dont think it can be fought
to a finish this fall.

I havent yet got that box you mailed Aug 10
and was about giving it up until today
when Tom Walker told me he just received

a box mailed July 7th, a jar of strawberries in it.
They hadnt put the wire clip over the cover –
well the strawberries had run all through

and spoiled it. A shame to throw it all away.
The first of the week I saw a play,
"Lucky Durham." The main thing is to have

the parts well acted. I suppose I wont
be satisfied to see moving pictures.
Plays will be apt to spoil me.

I heard a fine illustrated lecture on Pompeii,
Rome and Naples. The lecturer had a lantern
with slides, views all down the west coast of Italy,

Vesuvius. Nearly all the beauty of Europe
isnt natural, but the work of man. Very different
from the beauty of America. I want to see

more of America, if I can arrange to
without too much trouble.
The Hotels Cecil and Savoy on the Strand

are the best hotels in London. I wasnt in them
but on the grounds around them.
I would like to spend about 24 hours

in one. When we get to our new camp
we will all have heavy horses.
The worst part is cleaning the harness,

all the steel will have to be kept shining.
One is apt to have a few tumbles at first
over the jumps. The weather changes very quick –

one can never tell in the morning what kind of day
it will be. Oh how are the apples this year.
Have they had a very large crop.

Sometimes I sit in one of the chairs
in front of the fireplace – they have been keeping
a fire lately – and go over the times we had

in my mind. I would like to farm just as we did
but there will have to be some change.
It won't do for Dwight and I to go on working

together. That will have to be settled later.
The first thing for me to take a hand in settling
is this business over here.

One Bedroom Apartment

> For still temptation follows where thou art.
> – Sonnet 41, William Shakespeare

i

What Tempest Within

Unlooked-for flash –
                    the flesh, a room revealed
by lightning not misunderstood as fire
but sound. The rain was thunder not desire
as nails it drove in hard through shingles sealed
against entry, the little tongues of steeled
disaster you and I could not aspire
to turning sharp away from, bloodless, mire
us still, unthoughtful one-night love
                              – annealed.

The dulling storm undulls the cooling brain.

We lie apart unspent and silent, loud
with words unmouthed, our bodies' residue
unsafe evaporating slicks that stain
not just the arid sheets but skins, our shroud
of vapid sweat from which unfeeling flew.

ii

From a Portfolio of Japanese Erotic Prints

Of vapid sweat from which unfeeling flew
you blow me slow, attentive eyes not shut
so jarred, I jerk awake at noon, your blue
unquestioned stare inclined to move from nut

to hip, its line inscribed in spry woodcut
metrics up my torso to lips and brow
till I can't turn my gaze from yours, my butt
ensnared in dampened linens, cracked window

agape behind your head – a jack-pine bough
averse with wet it shakes through summer screens
in place beyond the snows, I note, till now –
unloosed by storm – the way my body leans

inside your own, a woodcut graven fresh
of men, unknown before, who fast enmesh.

iii
Maj. Tom's Cyberspace Oddity

Of men unknown before who fast enmesh
I know not one with candid eyes like yours
remorseless guys who come online, not flesh

but gigabytes; each .gif they post downpours
a faceless shard of fuzzy body parts
through wastes of RAM, as, lost, it meteors

a falling asteroid of REM that charts
deleted longing. Mine, theirs – should you care?
Such chance unseen trajectories none imparts

with thought, all inner space a web of rare
and rude replies or worse: utter dead air –
empathic vacuums far from debonair

until your squirt of queries coursed with flair –
your sleeve rolled up, my tattooed heart aware.

iv
Peter Fonda and Me

Your sleeve rolled up, my tattooed heart aware –
with opened eyes we know what flesh may tell
if nothing else. Our engines, revving, blare
essential anguish, rank desire, such hell
the freedom we discharge as bikers jacked
before we join, angst blown off as hapless
roadkill, tongues hit then run, detouring tact
two men who ride without aim, helmetless

before the big easy downpours and comes
to ground, every belvedere a plateau
while, snarled as rucked-up sheets, prairie succumbs
to flat horizon, scrub unfurled below
once scored by ecstasy, the skid we leave
careless transcript injurious to grieve.

v
Cavafy's Blinds, An Hour Open

Careless transcript injurious to grieve
I scan your skin before you dress, its pores

erased from dawn's recall, the airy sleeve
of night you wore now torn by what restores

ennui with raised-up shades, to flood naive
through sheers my tuneless solitude abhors –

such marbled abs as yours now find reprieve
from white, still drying inks my tongue adores

but no longer tastes, clothes zipped back on, bed
remade, the ceiling's gloom a sheet unshaped

by unsubtle forms once you leave; my head
vacates this room's undreamed-of guests inscaped

as blanks, as I am blank, your likeness fled
and me not clear if light or love escaped.

vi
Donne In

And me not clear if light or love escaped
the crown you deigned to wear a cast-off ring
you slipped, once flaccid, wholly free, its sting
elliptic, first and least; transcendence gaped
without savior, my gifts unwanted, scraped
from thighs despite such lived-out fantasies.
Unholy pipe dreams of which neither breathes
a word – our acts persist: they might be taped.

Or has perversion jaundiced me?
                     Who lifts
my yellowed soul from unwashed sheets no one
lies in once you roll away from spendthrift's
unmeaning spray? Its pouring forth has done
me in; little I care for seems the same –

may no desire in sorrow drown in shame.

vii
Like Crane's Heart, Abridged

May no desire in sorrow drown in shame.

The paling dawn may bronze the leaves outside
my dazzled window while street lamps elide
with day as you stroll away, your frame
less transparent than the rains that claim
reflection, your unlooking eyes at sea
in me – or will you turn and raise, in free
harbour, your hand and wave? Our span no shame
if brief.
                Two men join and ghost cities form
from Brooklyn past the Lion's Gate (pain healed
by Erato's traffic), this frenzied norm
of comrades like us becalmed, a link steeled
in beds by wireless pixellated storm –
unlooked-for flash
                the flesh
                        a room revealed.

The Roll Call to the Ark

> Was it that He said a pair

was it that He said seven pairs

> If it was a pair

if it was seven pairs

> Then what of those un-hatched

what of those fledglings

> What of inbreeding

souls and souls of silent sameness

> If it was a pair

if it was seven pairs

> Then let's start here

start with the lesser tit, the bearded

> With the Golden Eagle, the Imperial

does He care how they are named

> Does He care if they are beautiful

He does

> They are

the sparrow

> The Griffon Vulture

the golden oriole

> The Peregrine

does He care how they stand

> So proud, such long thin necks

so small, such plumage

> The Hoopoe, The Snow

finch, the skylark

> Did His friend gather

the eggs of the robin, the dove

> Crow, Raven eggs

did he eat any of them

> Did he crack them over a fire

feed them to his sons

                        Feed them to his sons' wives

and how did he house them

                        In the ribs of a cypress

in an aviary of dream

                        For the Little Owl

for the tree pipit

                        Did he take the seeds of trees

did he take branches

                        Foliage

some arching trunk

                        Was it crowded with still eyes

was it loud with tweets and twitters and tittering

                        Did the sons

did the wives

                        Threaten to hunt

yell out amid eternal headaches

                        How

how

                        Did they gather

that small-winged

                        Those sharp-clawed

the goldcrest

                        The Fisher-Owl

and what did they eat

                        Did he build a lake

did he build a forest

                        Did he let them out

did they feed on fruit

                        Clean the flooded lands

clean the fly-laden tables

                        Of the ripening flesh

of the overripe rinds and cores

                        Did He ponder

did He consider
> The length and breadth

the tiny-ness
> Of The Harpy Eagle

the bee humming bird
> Its taller-than-man wing span

its eggs smaller than the smallest finger nail
> Its potential to catch up

its potential to hide
> Did He consider

did He ponder
> Hand-sized talons

all the tiny hiding places
> Claws the length of a grizzly's

the arctic tern's yearly flight around the world?

TIM BOWLING

The Book Collector

for Harry Elkins Widener (1885–1912)

I have less than twenty-seven minutes to write this poem
about Harry Elkins Widener who drowned
on the *Titanic* April 1912 with or without
his recently-purchased second edition (1598)
of Bacon's *Essais* which, romantic accounts
insist, he leaped out of a lowering lifeboat
to retrieve, less than twenty-four minutes now
to tell you I've struck a seemingly benign iceberg
in my life and I'm hastily yet tenderly
ushering the consequential memories
into the ice-jagged sea and standing back
as the ropes creak and my father's
pipe smoke aspires with the hymns
to a heaven almost universally believed in,
eighteen minutes to acknowledge the death
of youth's purchase, seventeen minutes
to blink at my mother's diminishing shade
as the china slides and crashes
and the crushed velvet in the ballroom
loses forever the echo of the steps
of the past. An old man cries
composedly, and out of the dark
a woman shrieks words in the just-learned
tongue of terror, I am down to twelve minutes
and what am I going to say to you,
stowaways at the rail of another's heart,
that can bring you faster across
the killing waters? I must address
myself instead to the running-out sand
in the glass of Harry Elkins Widener

who did not live to spend the whole
of the family fortune on Shakespeare Folios
and Gutenberg Bibles but slipped into
the relentlessly clattering
press of tragedy and history
and became blank, void
as the sea and the sleepless hours
of the woman who bore him. Harry,
I have six minutes, and after them
I will live, I will walk in this body
on the earth as the iceberg
that will kill me bows and
retracts like a dancer from your era
to wait in the wings for ten
or twenty or forty years,
but tell me, what is the material
to what can only be, at essence,
spirit? Should I in my dwindling minutes
divest myself of the armature
of belief in printed expression to succor
and sustain? Three minutes. Two.

Young Mr. Widener, Sir,
you didn't go back for the book,
you didn't even think of it
or of Shakespeare or Gutenberg
as the ship tilted like a parched throat
beneath a cracked glass. Romance
is a luxury of the living and you
were several staircases down on your way to death,
and we who have made a start behind you,
gathering and spending, turning the rare pages
with delight, shelving and reshelving
the accumulated wisdom

of the world, adherents
to the faith in permanence,
sniff the Alexandrian smoke
and turn over in our first-class berths
and steerage bunks or play
another hand of poker
as the lights flicker
and at last go out.

This is the final moment
of the final poem of my youth
which will be printed and bound
between covers and found perhaps
by others as I found your name, Harry,
by the serendipity of our common passion
for the rescue ship to arrive in time
and the tragedy to be told as comedy
by firelight some far-off year.

Goodbye, Harry. Goodbye who you were,
who I was, who we all were.
Peace to your unrecovered bones,
the hours lived.
Peace to the eternal ligatures.

One of us is in a Mohawk cemetery

It was another pleasant
afternoon near the river.
There was supper in the slow cooker
and nothing was curled in the storm sewer.
A dog barked Blue Sky two times.
It was a semiotic moment you said. Then you said
actually more 'pataphysical.
And to let myself in I said Meta Meta
Met a man with seven wives. But you
were daydreaming about some girl. I knew
you didn't hear me. Ears are too close to brain.
One newly buried mother leads to another
and ours are eternally elsewhere. Have you ever
loved anything more? Didn't you?
I will warn you: I don't know these mushrooms
and you could wait all summer for someone
to lean into your life.
Or just say Me Me.
I stand corrected: You You.

Stars, Sunday Dawn

Declination: the angular distance of a star, north or south of a celestial marker.

Mornings, the boy is down the stairs before he knows it. The body
    leading.
A banister of hours beneath his hands. Habit has no need of light in
    halls –
above, below – the width of oriental runners. Their import worn –
    ravelled
by the circuit he's made of every surface. Each room, a perimeter of
    breath.

Blur of tartan over the newel post, rakish skid, and he's where I wait:
parlour, window-starting bright – glazed trees and beyond a band
of violet clouds girdling the horizon – stars paling on a victor's belt.

All this he sees, ignores,
              the spinning boy, my brother,
                           for whom the day's a stadium.

The granary – I need you to see this – an amphitheatre of yellow
    chaffy light.
The bins of grain are up the wooden stairs; the crusher's chute, the
    only thing below.
Where wagons wait, or will, when day is fully come. Bran or
    middlings,
depending on the setting of the gears. Grinding days, all but Sunday.
A wall calendar for figuring, tacked on a two-by-four. The planets in
    their courses.

It's here, he explains the dividend of seconds; sometimes, the
    escapement of a watch.
Too young to read, I'd read its face a hundred times, and his – its
    fractional fury every dawn.
Lapsed time, he says, equates to distance: start to finish. Flight of
    thought between.
He's got his helmet hat on, the ear flaps tied behind like usual.
                                     Its leather cracked with time.

A declination, I think, is what I'd name it now, that interval from
    there to here.

For some, the poem's a timepiece, a repeater watch. The one who
    watches
hauls out of harm's way a Sunday boy who hadn't breath for common
    days.

Last One on the Moon

How could something so rote,
so written, find time to surprise?
Niche of cliché, nemesis of fresh,
yet there it is again, lording it over the
firing dust, silhouettes of trees...
Never agreed to be extras, never think of
themselves as frames, never thought a thing
except in this drowsy context, which
morphs into heartfelt syntax, scares that
cynic heart you worship straight.

It's not that you want to stand up there
(you do), it's that it stands you up
in an uncomfortable cold that's always
cold now, on a bike, on a bike path
pressing down, beside a highway suddenly
tragic without its pointless imagined
lunar road signs... panting over
spinning wheels, which have never
in your experience struck you as ancient
or orbital, though they are now as
surely as they won't be tomorrow.

Perhaps it speaks to childhood: last one
on the moon's a rotten egg, lost morning,
poor reflection of what happened here
just twenty-one seconds ago, right here beside
you, and bounced back. Wrong? Sure.
Terracentrically incorrect. Any light in that
gray eye could only be the fireball itself.

A Walker in the City

Astringent day in early winter
when all the angels have been let out
of their cages. The wet blue beak
of morning, sky skidding on ahead

or flying – the sky – *flying* laundry.
Shunting cirrus back and forth (sky)
swerving its tracks boing-boing
rubber as a ball highing

the bluest bit of hush at the centre
of a jaunty girl's jaunty eye.
Caloo Calay, arias she out (but soft
away). Then shining all

and sure vaults she the wind's
cathedral stamping booted feet
lifting a hand unmittened, yes,
the better to balance welterweight

wind (flying fists) on a wet fingertip.
Hello again, hello. It's me (it's only me).

*

City bristlin' gloves today, handless,
cut off at the wrist. That's
supplication at best, at worst
the bait 'n grab of a supple leather

up-yours beneath her seat on the no. 61
uptown. As blue as that mitten
flashfrozen into prayer on this morning's
path. Yes, gloves gathering

in all the world's soiled places
where she's too long stared
herself down. Dear termagant,
like all collectors despairing

the end of the collection. Left
hand to match bleating calfskin
(no. 5 ½) or missing hand-
combed angora in damson

and plush. Brisk brisk, a walker
in the city, stoops & strides, blush
blush away, glove clutched jittery
in hand, hand in hand.

            *

That girl again, ho! A walker
in the city measures distance in feet
defeats lengthening lamppost gaps,
width of a line scrawled

on a hasty page. As if walking
merely to conjugate the season's
crackling yellow declensions.
But winter now… winter

and the world funnels inwards,
declines, ah, elegant
within cagey astrakhan, between
closed lids, lips. Let's

catch her, moth-girl, against the lit
page, against flying leaves
herself, selving, angular & awkward.
Girl with a name like a shrug,

a one-handed wave, terse
in the flyleaf of some book
of posthumous queries. *How many
shoes did Dante wear out*

while writing the Commedia?
Breathes she a prayer (a curse)
cast visible in discrete
indiscreet puffs before sweeping

to heaven on an updraft. Meanwhile
thighs she hard and trim
the street to her stride, alive
alive-o! A spasm of *agape*

gaping open in her throat
and morning
swinging sideways, flaring open
with her coat.

*

Like the last of the summer bees,
dazed, dashing for hothouse interiors
bumbling the pockets of windbreakers,
satchel linings. This longing

for God that springs unholy water
gushing to the mouth as if
at the scent of meat grilling. Every year
'round this time summer tenses

past, a frantic bird flying
out of her mouth, flying south. Well-cut
eyes, curt temples: she loses
her temper more & moreish, allowing

thus everyone else to keep theirs.
Darkens, then, penitential violets
beneath her eyes. The people in this city
like strike-on-anything matches,

blazing friendships on street corners,
in elevators. Ready to rub heads
with anyone, everyone, flaring briefly
in the dusk. Ah recompose

my disquiet. (Observe, watch
how she licks her fingers
between the pages of a book.) Look,
just as well considering the darkness

falls each year not all of which
can extinguish the light
from a single cigarette, not
all the darkness. One day

mid-winters she a fist, pocket-
deep. Pulls out, frail & brown,
blown, the corpse of a thought
lost months ago
                    buzz
                            buzz

          *

Comes the night and falls the snow.
That disproportion, snow,
resolved to perfect
the collapsing scaffold of winter.

Nothing else, not love or grief,
not anger or etiquette, Lordy, so
ex-*ces*-sive. That walker, mud-booted,
 her hands, her cheeks, cold

as allegory as – as
that which escapes comparison, *ha!*
Yea though she walks
cogitates she those honeycombed

lives. Lit windows, bent heads
absolving the dishes clean. Passes
the old city poet in his aerie
dismantled this night by lust

or virtue, pacing his rooms, scribbling
poems to his circling
unsuitable self. (Burning the topless
towers of Ilium and so forth, muttering

so? I misread the past. It was, after all,
a difficult book.) Come home, girl,
give us a kiss, do. Her fingers wet
and darkness falling

in decorous arches: tumbled, sprawling.

*

Hunched, hatching his little death
sits he, Brother Pig. That old poet all
squalorous and gone in the teeth
but the pitcher in him full or half

at least. A little leaking life, faith
and anti-faith hoarded equally, a loose
handful of words to turn the humming
world on its tilted ear, yas. Searches

for a word, a sentence takes off on its own,
joins someone else's poem.
So: walking girl leans windward, peels
nail polish in a thick rind, her long

nails clicking a tangerine rosary.
The old poet wonders what she looks like
(ah take this cup from my lips) does not
turn to belabour her points, charmed

by the coupla things already he knows.
As item: the unbroken
citrus curl. As item: a steady
devout click.

*

So, you think walking solves the world?
Cures what ails you? Nimbly she side-
steps his complex plaint, his inky
blue lines thrown out to reel

her in. The sky a soggy grey lung
overhead breathing *hoo*wah. Or no,
the winter sky snapping like bunting.
Either way comparisons evade

the subject, hasten to miss their
appointments. Lacking curves the way rivers
lack angles. His baited prose, I mean, his eye
tuned to the hazy blue frequencies

of distance. Ago and much ago
she was his once upon
a much ado – about nothing gave she quarter
and green grew the rushes-o!

*

So? She is a walker in the city,
of young & brimming age, so
suffers the streets to move through
her, to move her. The foot a precise

approximation of length. Like poetic metre
or the distance at any one radius
between two radiant lovers. Ah look what you
do done done to me! whistles he

through the sugar cube in his teeth, that old
reprobate, his currentless
amblings all over this page, his mindful
heart, his capital F for art

(its vectoring flight). The seen frothing up
at the intersection of object & gaze,
the glaze, the light. *The seen*
leaking out of his eyes in cataracts.

*

Westward ho ho ho. Trudgy with weariness
off the gimlet shift and longing
for the vicious rounding of a little sleep.
But how to get home again, homesweet

east-best and wee wee wee (all the way).
And she without her wings, without key
or compass or ruby mittens. She lost. Alas,
alack lacks she volition, verily

so tired, you see. Mired in the high
mucky-muck of toil & trouble, wan
and wondering, by the bus stop palely loitering.
Who owns this night the city?

Grain merchants, oilers and bankers, cutpurses,
rogues. I trow, some slithy tove
or other in an office tower 'bove Portage & Main.
The golden lad highballing his legislature

or Worm the Conqueror? She walks
to disown. The Möbius spool

to spool of earth & sky, no joints showing
unpremeditated snowing

and then the lighting of the lamps.

*

Blinks the hazy orange eye
of a no. 18 cross-town in which an old party
cable-knitted to a flecked rectitude
faces inwards profiling his spruce coin.

Above her dozy lapse
the Heinz baby food baby
agape with joy. Mood Gush
to the Last Spoonerism! Gathers the bus

and rattles them as stones into
one pocket: an old man, tired girl, that beamish
tot shiny as pate. Full
holy at last, one family, at least

for another two stops. Advertisement
for Madonna & Child, St. Joseph gazing
        benignly on
while the past tenses – perfects itself
in the future's radiant pigment. What the city

offers tentatively, tenderly,
late at night and far away from home:
a stone in the shoe, the body's thin metal-
fatigued chrome, presentiment of kin

between strangers.

*

Fall, season of the *döppelganger*, that unhoused
girl who straggles behind
kicking leaves at his ankles. Wherever he goes
she follows, his canny adjective.

Give me a name, she begs, *and I'll leave.* Leaves,
autumn cut-outs
peel like decals from the illustrative elms.
Also, the matter of his sour

mood, snarling at smokers, coughers,
falterers between one step,
the next. And those who mumble
directions, palate banality, who knock

green apples against their teeth (*crisply*
on the bus) who fumble change
in the post office line. More or less,
these days and then less and less.

*

A name, a name, she prods
nose buried in tracts of fur
forty nylons once were slaughtered
to provide. Share they the wind,

the sky. Share they a fumbly history
of the knocks and falters a city delivers
in the course of a morning, say, skittering
on thin-skinned ice. Share they

wind-caper, sun-spin. Like him
she is a walker in the city. Advance,
advance: they avoid as passersby avoid
each other's glance.

*

Tis the season of packing up and digging in,
tis the season of being done. *Tis the day
after twas*, he doggerels in the margin
of a notebook, foxed endpapers

and vellumish pages like a Madonna
with a hundred white hands
folded shut. Ah, but what
what to do with her, where to escort her,

this walker? Wants to write until she comes
home to him, his walker, mud-
booted, her hands her cheeks cold as air.
They share eyes, *unheimlich*

manoeuvre, blue snap of shadow across
alluvial snow. So –
so: a name like an indrawn breath, *cara
mia*. Easing her narrow shoulders

into the unused day, heave and hawk,
bulging to swallow a sip, a crumb.
A word smooth and oval as a pill – love,
say, or pain – gulped down

with the morning coffee. Give me
a name, she pants. Beside herself.

*

Cara mia, mea culpa. My darling, my fault.
(His fortunate importunate
fall.) Or consider static, a well-fed refrigerator
ruminating on its appetites.

Think of all those buzzing words
flashed down to a green asterisk
centre of a blank afternoon: Mia, mine.
Centring the true of noon. As in:

whene'er in furs my Mia goes
then wakes she stars like footnotes
to the planets discord. As in:
two walkers walking beneath high

crackling winds. As in: one following
or (to reverse the vice) one leading.
Caught like socks in the hot drum
of a dryer. Clinging statically,

ecstatically. Flashing blue into
true poetry. (And what about static
poems, hmm? Words that
crackle, words that cling?)

Felix and Mia
walking the pr-air-ie
C. U. S. S. I. N. G.

wind catspawed his jowl / her little cheek, pat pat

*

That dawning moment when the world,
framed in glass, enters the window pane.
Good morrow, waking soul! Mia wakes
hasty as a dreamer baulked

by impossible metre. Nothing rhymes,
for example, orange. On subject of which
was colour named for fruit or fruit
brute colour? A walker wakes, trailing

two fingers through wake
of sleep, aah... One of those
sudsy dreams drains thick & slow
leaves lime stains and hard

water deposits on the inside of the mind.
Lint, lint... a day (when she steps foot)
one stride or breath, too wide, too small.
Eventually all acorns fall, wing & root

from chicken-little skies. On subject of which
does left mean wrong? Can one begin
an autobiography without believing
the end of the story? On subject

of which what ebbs & flows from grief,
what wanes? And what
did dreamers dream before the invention
of tunnels and their trains?

Union Station

I cannot love you all and I won't.

The shoulder knows the will of the heart and its way around
a crowd. The clam-soft give. The crack of the shell.

Help me recognize your humanity – talk in a low slow voice,
wave your lunch bone arms.

The children with keys at collarbone are building fires
in the tunnels, forts at every junction.

Let them go. The way is littered with leftovers –
pale white stalks, tender volva. Pick one. Another.

There are other ways home.

Brushed metal canines, the gate, will score
what you can afford to leave behind.

Impress me with your stones, your height.
The sweet dip of your neck.

All that you love,
keep high.

There, there

Poppies are tap-rooted and do not take well to transplanting, so sow the seeds
in flowering position in early spring.
– Florabunda Seeds Catalogue, 2005

Then it was April. We'd set all our clocks to the future.
It was the last of first and last, the month to ask
the liquor store for boxes. Then to suture up the past,
to set each step down like a stitch, and lay
a nurse-like hand on what we'd miss. I took a spade
and scraped the dirt, unsure if you were salt
or spirit in my fist. Dry whispers as you shifted,
claws on branches, tongue-tied clicks, as if upon release
you'd scatter into crows. But you dropped,
my loose vaccine for grief. That day was rehearsal.
Later, I would blink my shutter eyelids at the house and drive
as if the truck were band-aid – *one clean pull* –
I'd need you then, unfolding, comma of root and leaf.

Blindness

The barn is ripe with geldings and mares;
how well they get along without
the bother of balls and fidelity.
The one stallion snorts by the far door,
as if disgusted by the easy
equanimity, knocking the gate
with his hammer hooves, letting everyone
know they're unsafe. A sheen of nervousness
in the air, flecks of hay drifting
in the sliced sunbeams like tiny flares.
Except for Sprout, across the way,
one of the castrati, whose head-bends
beg a bold friendliness. From the left,
he's suede and apple butter, with
an emperor's snout, a profile
fit for a coin. But seen from the right,
he becomes a missing eye, a long-
ago accident, as if a cage
had lost its golden bird, or a shrine
its simple saint. Gruesome, perverse,
the worst thing you'll see today. Wouldn't
blame you if you ran, muck flicking
from the soles of your shoes. But of course,
you'll stay, the empty socket of your will
reminding you of how distorted
you often feel. Just your heart
alone is an ugly mess;
if anyone ever really took the time
for a good look. And so you ease closer,
Sprout nodding, urging you in. He breathes
the back of your neck, then lowers himself
into a nuzzle, left side first, then

right, oh, Christ, here it comes, the accident
that never ends, the loneliness that
reminds you how much you need to be seen.
The barn goes dark and light in separate
strips, a pattern you'd once have thought
was choice. This time though you touch it all,
the bronze flanks, the shady fringe of mane,
the nothingness that narrows to
an incandescent finger, finally
entering the loss. Sprout whinnies,
less alone now, as close to loved
as shock can get. You stake a foothold
in the straw and shit, and stare up at him,
all flinches fled. Blindness, so soft
and eager, it almost talks.

The Gift

The streets flooded by people watching an apartment fire.
The Klu Klux white dress she wore. The weather's rigmarole.
The silver hero in the clouds. The galvanizing. The franchise.
The bright backwash. The hollow village. The weather's rebuttal.
The throat-cut rooster, its beak wide with crow.
The mule train bringing a piano through scrub-brush.
The dwarf pines. The winterkill. The birch-knots in the stove.
The waft as souvenir. The ripe lanterns in the orchard.
The crinoline lakes. The drowned lollystick legs.
The fishnets. The doldrums. The wanderlust. The Duchess.
The gramophone's tin ear. The carriage road.
The leaf mould. The unexploded ordinance. The bloom.
The small arms fire. The child fire. The sightlines.
The dooryard. The courtlight. The wraith-sparrows.
The swagger. The little something to cut the dust.
The carbines. The Admirals niece in oilskins.
The understudy who runs away with his wife.
The regency. The deadweight. The bedside telephone.
The stairs down the bluffs. The Empress on the pebble beach.
The moulting snakes. The wildfowl. The caverns.
The names run down by their echo.
The piano so immaculate it must be hollow.
The hawthorn belt around her muslin dress.
The jackdaws. The peck horns. The silverfish.
The dust-dulled brass. The rabbit-punch.
The wicker traps. The overcoat gone to seed.
The boozy weave of a grackle off the pane.
The same thin richness of these worlds remain.
The cavalcade along her legs. The coronation.
The cannonade of hailstones on the xylophones.
The pterodactyl of silence that follows.

[* The italicized line is from Peter Porter's poem "John Marston Advises Anger".]

Museum

> But one writes only after one has willed to renounce the will, and the wisest of
> poets have always insisted that in the long run all poetry that is worth listening
> to has been written by the gods.
> – Northrop Frye

Subway, in the middle of my commute,
  I found myself in a dark corner.
The line vanished into the underground
  in two directions, the clack and crow-screech

of steel wheels echoed in recession
  of the just missed five-o-nine
from the tunnel's depths. Museum Station.
  A chilled solitude widened around me

and water-drops pooled in mimicked snips
  between the rails below. The ceiling lamps'
subdued fluorescence seemed to cast no shadows
  and were like peering through green water.

Exhibits from the ROM in glass cases
  with aboriginal wooden masks descended
like messengers from the real world above,
  whose outsize faces gestured witness and alarm

in the apocalyptic style of indigenous myth.
  Farther up, the February dusk
was tawny, the air tasteless and dull
  as pewter plate. Fog had moved in on

Old Vic's scrubbed-stone but now vague
    turrets uncobbling upwards to the last
vanished spire, as though parting illusion
    from the epigraph above the stairway arch,

still insisting, after these twenty years,
    that the truth would set me free.
All gone up in a mist now, as far
    as I could see. I pictured them above,

the Burwash quad, Pratt, and residence,
    whose faux-gothic walls hold the city at Bay
like the brim of an empty cup, and where
    the mind-set of college years, memories

of what unwritten words, burn perpetually
    as in a crucible. I wonder now had I known,
those years hiding my fidgets, of the tics
    Touretters spend their days trying to release,

or heard of how the obsessive's repetitions
    grind every last impulse to its death,
would I have finished more, managed
    the regimental *habitus* and got things done?

Too skittish by far to do as that passage
    from Faust always roared mockingly I should,
from its perch on the cork board above my desk,
    Settle your studies! and sound the depths

of that thou wilt profess. Get real! I still
    have the welts from the nightly tongue-lashing.
But now school's out at last, and the long ghostly
    hours of doodling, daydreams, lectures, lessen.

The students pouring from Northrop Frye Hall
   slushed in out of the fog in private directions
escalating down into the commuter scrimmage
   towards the platform. And that brought it on.

The clapping heel, nasal-snort, the lurching nod,
   the whooped-up screech and cluck.
I tried to catch the right patterns up,
   send them unfolding in dervish rhythms,

unstoppable as blinking. Suddenly,
   out of the unasked-for corporal hootenanny
I sensed a conjured presence whirled out
   in tangents from myself echoing

in the sniggers I bounced off the walls,
   until in my thinking, it appeared,
a stooped man stood apart,
   behind a pillar, unhurried, thoughtful,

neither leaving nor arriving, one I seemed
   to recognize or remember, coming through
and breaking up like a cell-phone signal
   too far from its source. The chunky glasses

and electric hair, plain, perennially ancient,
   he was there, bunched up within himself
like New Brunswick brushwood, swaying
   like a scraggly jack-pine or as a man

in thought at arm's length from a lectern
   will rock, it seems, to captivating rhythms
for the sake of argument. Sheet folder.
   Waiting for this line to take him home.

He spoke up under my own chirps and wheens
  snickering back under the stone work,
like a cold draft working itself out.
  "Still conjuring ghosts, are you Hamlet,

from the depths of the waiting place?
  Have you forgotten my Shakespeare lecture
in '81, on how the Danish spook
  is not one jot less real than the made world

he rises in?" He looked himself over.
  "Not that I can say much in the matter,
but you might have made me younger.
  When you conjure someone in a dream,

(where *are* your manners?) it's best to be more
  generous than time was.... But look at *you*.
Why you look as though you see a burning
  bush or a hanging disk of fire."

"Oh no no, I see you, heavenly ghost,
  old sky father, old officer of art!
but holy company of angels
  what are you doing here? Fifteen years

have passed since we sat through the Blake
  readings at your remembrance service,
and together cracked what wine bottles afterwards
  launched you on your way across the Styx,

that second journey you once wrote about
  as having rather less to do with ego
than the first. You always looked for how
  to get past it without actually dying,

and I thought if I kept reading your prose
   you might show the way chosen ones take
to the spiritualized secular,
   and find you again, or myself at least.

But not haunting some in-transit concourse
   buried under old grounds I've already trod."
"You're still looking in all the wrong places.
   Time you saw through your own smoke and mirrors."

"A window then? Not a thing I see?"
   "Closer, yes, but don't get your hopes up
on clarity, too many hands and noses
   have been pressed to the glass for you to find

what you're looking for in someone like me,
   even in this state. I was never much
for small talk, as little on subway platforms
   as on that elevator we once rode together."

He shied away three steps and started to fade,
   searched himself as for the rumpled coat
he was still wearing. But I wanted more,
   moved to step clear of my own withholdings.

"I've long imagined I had missed my chance,
   had lost you to the ranks of bygone
paternal mentors, fathers in whom I planted
   the seeds of long-nursed dependencies

for the tall harvest that never came."
   "Still stripping grafts from confidences
greater than your own? You've a way to go,
   and it won't be this old crow, cocking

his eye at you under these shady lights,
 who will get you there. Don't you know
that mine too was the ventriloquist's thrown voice,
 and that what I spoke was a stirred echo?"

"I'll never write as much as you did, spirit,
 the endless notebook-drafts of plumbed inklings
and the thirty odd volumes of limpid prose.
 I can't pinch off a dozen lines in a year."

"You could use some metaphoric roughage
 in your diet. An evacuation and purge,
as Auden said, can be a positive omen.
 But you're the one who goes on about Whitman....

You have to keep the tics down in public,
 and the vocal dirt from passing at all times,
(like Kegel exercises for the mental sphincter...).
 I can understand that. But your verbal

warm-ups are over-worked, if I may say so,
 too handled and pushed, too proudly shaped.
You'd rather lay off the inkpot than risk
 the odd bad sheet, won't commit a line

not already hammered into its promise.
 You have this chiselled-phrase stuff backwards.
A poet finishes with cut gems
 for the jeweller's eye, his sturdy maxim's

sculpted waterfall hefted upwards
 into empyrean, he doesn't start there.
You're a Touretter. Why not write like one?
 Hold off the perfectionist blocking out phrases

to exhaustion, those worrying threads,
    the Penelopian back-ravellings of the unmade.
Your repetitious tics have always come first,
    and so they should, the ecstatic rhapsodist's

St. Vitus Dance, slangster's whizzle
    and conjuration, philologist's hullaballoo.
You think of Moses breasting the mountain top
    to find the right words *already* carved

in stone. But Moses too went round and round,
    'til he found the clearing and the words came."
My tics slowed, and he dimmed like a science fair
    light bulb, whose frail filament is

kept lit by the frantic, pumping cyclist
    'til he tires. I cried, "But wait! What words?
Suppose I do dance circles, make off-beat
    tongue-claves my first exuberance, tell me

what I'll find there *beyond*." "No time," he said,
    turning away, "and we've both said enough.
But look, you've waited on this line for some time,
    haven't you. I think I hear what you need coming,"

he said, and fading, said something else I missed,
    when a shriek, as from depths within, drowned him out,
and it was then I saw, what else?, a light
    at the end of the tunnel, and heard the train's

sliced-steel, involuntary skreak and howl,
    an offense to all, but look with how many
along for the ride! One last tic, I sounded
    my barbaric yawp. And a door opened.

Box

Big enough for me to crawl into. It might've held
a fake Christmas tree, neighbour's TV or holiday
imperishables from the Sally Ann.
I was ten, making a house in the living room.

Cut out a window, opened a door. "Look at my box"
I called to my mother, and her friend put down his drink,
chided, half-slurred, "Don't say that," in a tone
that begged me to ask why. "Don't say

that" he said again. And in the pause
while he raised his glass in slow-mo and drank,
eyeing me, I sat back on my heels and glimpsed
the fourth wall, a spare self watching a trashy play.

"Cut it out" my mother said, "she's just a kid," swatting
the wasp after the sting. "I'm just a fucking drunk," his line.
Everything doubled, obscene, sublime –
No safety in words, then. And more room.

Spineless Sonnet

Your forearm supplies the sock puppet's spine,
your thoughts checker the sock's, your will argyles
the plain white weave. The sock's got half a mind –
though one half too few – to refuse to smile,
and grins and bears the voices in its head:
your four fingers and opposable thumb
miming the mouthful that cannot be said.
Elastic resolve slackens, lips once mum
now loose and sinking ships. But its windows
to the soul, salvaged from snowmen's sockets,
stay sewn on. De-boned, it sways when wind blows
like reversed Depression-era pockets,
and dreams of ventriloquist's knees, a pawn's
wooden posture, just one leg to stand on.

Song of the Taxidermist

> Beauty is momentary in the mind,
>
> The fitful tracing of a portal,
> But in the flesh it is immortal.
> – Wallace Stevens

Grin, Niemeyer's Taxidermy, 2005.
Polyurethane bear mount.

It's best if they bring it in untouched –
most men are butchers with a knife.

All the wild resides in your garage, saved
for their racks, their teeth and fine plumage,

while just across the fields, where new stacks
aim skyward like smoking guns, everything

comes out dog food. Today a bear arrived
in a box: *See what you can do for him,* said

the owner as if to a doctor, the illness,
terminal: death by deflation. The trick is

knowing what he'd been up to the moment
he was surprised by a tingling in his neck.

You can't learn it in books. Even manikin
catalogues are recipes for still lives. Your

grandmother baked by weight, the taste of
rising dough. You know an eighteen-inch

neck just lifting a deer pelt from its box.
See it stretch to meet an itching hind hoof

in a logged clearing, the others sunk in
fireweed. *Shouldn't we all get a second*

chance at beauty? You squat between gallons
of bondo and borax, brushing the doe's

damp throat with your daughter's
brush, or it will dry like that, unnatural.

*

Relay, Niemeyer's Taxidermy, 2005.
Zebra legs in taxidermy.

These legs would do for table or footstool,
drag boots for women bent on animal

prints. I filled them with what was handy:
firewood from the slumping ravine.

Listen, we are all afraid of abandonment,
but there is nothing to be done.

Think of it as recycling grace. Villagers
thought I was spoiling good meat when I

fiberglassed a sable antelope from the
shoulders up, but they were wasting too:

no one remembers one meal from the next.
African sun putrefied the flesh scooped

out, but it mounted fine beside the moose
in my living room. Left to themselves,

legs are inclined to ramble on about hot
savannah, making thunder underfoot,

until they run out of words to describe:
herd, dance, smell of rain before it falls.

It is sight makes us stumble. Around us
are unbroken plains. Around us are crutches of

those who walked lightly away. I set to with
a buck saw because no one was using them,

and they were beautiful like that, bright
batons in my bag, the long flight home.

*

Zarafe, Muséum d'Histoire Naturelle de la Rochelle, 1845.
Giraffe in taxidermy.

You were famous eighteen years, Egypt's
ambassador to France. Modernism in

walking boots and yellow coat.
Balzac celebrated with a story and

Flaubert held his mother's hand before your
towering metaphor. All of Paris celebrated

polygons: everything "à la giraffe,"
women crouching on carriage floors to

preserve haute coiffure's new heights,
the winter flu your namesake. These days,

you keep company with Empress Josephine's
orang-utan, half a dozen shrunken heads,

stuffed with what you dreamed on in winter,
gold fields waving. You used to embody

the Nile, today it's our own past we're
spectating – not so much as a shirr

in the whole animal thanks to arsenic
and good upholstery. Come see the

original tall tale! The seven neck bones
we have in common, insomnia,

an awkward grace. Let's just say
we loved our wonder like teenagers

love vertigo, that's why you're here,
still standing in for something else.

*

7 leagues, Niemeyer's Taxidermy, 2005.
Elephant foot in taxidermy.

They say in war the most valuable thing
is a pair of good boots – when you fall

they're fair game, back and forth
without taking sides. No one will

bury it, the foot that is. A grave is
for head or heart – house of the eye,

transcriber of dreams, love's red
clutch – may they find rest. Consider

Riopelle's bestiary, all trunk and
ears and darkness below the body.

Our phantoms leave no tracks
by which to follow them home.

Put your ear to the ground, you'll
hear nothing but blood running.

*

Togo, Iditarod Trail Sled Dog Race Gift Shop / Museum, 1959.
Siberian Husky in taxidermy.

Here stands the carrier of the cure for
Diphtheria, like last summer's midway prize,

become his own memorial. Two hundred sixty
miles to Bluff in a blizzard – his would be the nose

to follow if the way before you turns to floes, or
a thousand snow geese take to the earth about

your feet. Heroism is measured in ground traversed,
the mercuric winds. Heihachiro Togo sunk the

Russians into the Baltic and became a Shinto kami.
His namesake plunged back into Artic waters to take

up his broken traces and pull the sled off Norton Sound,
the serum floating like bubbles in a carpenter's level.

To have such singular purpose! Just as surely, the
conditional anterior reeks up from under the fridge

after a free fall off the counter some months ago.
Regret runs in a pack, tongues lolling – who will

finish first? The same who calls up a storm every time
the door opens. What they don't tell is how Togo

escaped after the race to chase reindeer, returned to
the kennel just as satisfied. Does the wishbone

summon the impulse to pull apart, when we carry
all paths within us? Be wary of those that make

all the difference, monuments so surefooted
in the past, you'd think it were also cast.

*

Novecento, Maurizio Cattelan, 1997.
Horse in taxidermy with sling.

Instead of boiling down to gelatin,
you swing like a trapeze artist over

the heads of shrieking children. This
is our craft: take a skin and fill it to

the ears with rumination. It will
collect dust somewhere before being

thrown out, soaked up by the garden
like coffee grounds, baiting worms

in the moist earth whose gift is infinite.
Still, not every sparrow's flight is useful,

but is tribute to the afternoon off the
cliffs where the wind throws you for

a loop. Transfixed, sky and earth
stretch your legs like compass

needles north. See, even the moon is
a hoof print on the darkening shore.

*

Natures Mortes: Portrait de Cézanne/Portrait de Renoir/Portrait de Rembrandt, Francis Picabia,
1920. Monkey in taxidermy, nails, board, paint.

You're the original still life, nailed
like Curious George to a board.

With this tail, you motion, *I'll
colour your world.* You were

supposed to be caught playing
in the garden, but it's just as well

because you can't hold a pose
around fruit. It's not about you

anyway, you're an exclamation
mark: art is more like the real

world if it's made of the real
world. Trucks shake the street

according to their weight, the
cantaloupe in its bowl collects

flies. You smile at my profile
against the open window. Light

reaches us equally. For the moment,
nothing happens.

*

Monogram, Robert Rauschenberg, 1959.
Angora goat in taxidermy, tire, police barrier, heel of a shoe, tennis ball, oil, metal, wood,
fabric, paper, canvas, and wooden platform mounted on casters.

After four years loitering about the studio,
you gave him a canvas to stand on and seeded

it with urban debris. Be natural, you said, think
of the tire around you as a swing, a portal to

greener pastures. Then you splashed paint
on his face and brushed the treads white, as

if he'd been rolling across the surface of the
moon. We were fed up with illusions and

enigmatic grins. A goat was just what was
needed, something you could grab by the

beard, ride if necessary. When you found
him stuffed on 23rd Street, you were looking

for a new way to paint, to force materials to
speak for themselves. Now, he's an advocate for

the age of juxtaposition. Personally, I prefer
holding the past accountable – your father one

evening with blood on his hands, your mother's
silent apology gives him away. *It's not a dog,*

he says, and you bay at the door closing on
your childhood, its billy ears.

*

L'Homme à la mandibule, 1776–1781. Honoré Fragonard.
Skinned cadaver with donkey jawbone.

> The painter who has acquired the knowledge of the nature of the sinews,
> muscles and tendons will know exactly in the movement of any limb how many
> and which of the sinews are the cause of it...
> – Leonardo da Vinci

i

Draw the skin like a curtain spotlighting the
body's constant grin. Map its veins with wax

and alloys, dress it in a lacquer coat to make a
human window. What do you see? The seat

of reason is the mass of a cabbage; as of birth the
fist grows in tandem with the heart until it shakes

in traffic jams at cars cutting in, or sits in the lap like
a dying bird, sunspotted. This is cold Science and

students will benefit from such precision. Anatomy
is the sum of its parts: the room is white, the coats

and tiles so that even shadows are accounted for.
You are brother to the famous painter, the pedant

in the family, but have no illusions about art.
Anyone can see there are other possibilities

for each natural occurrence. You take your
scalpel and consider where to begin.

ii

L'homme 1149 is of average height with good
musculature, a manual labourer, used to gripping

tools and taking orders. You open him like a
welder the hull of a ship, or something burrowed

out – bees in the carcass of a lion, jugulars
flapping bootlaces, trapezius and deltoid uprooted

saplings. Ears and lips shrivel into a snarl, the sunken
nose, jutting penis; eleven operations by candlelight

to give the body back its natural poise because we're
not made of clay with its riverbank way of giving

in when pressed. Flesh remembers how it pulled
the bones out of bed in the morning, punched a kid

on the bridge after the heat wave, rain and blood
sweet relief – even here on a table in this cold room.

iii

Give a man a sceptre to rouse a king, a scroll
to make a scholar. You grant him the jawbone

of an ass and summon up the original hulk. Behold
the berserker, a handy fellow in a tight spot,

swinging his bone around like a scyther in the field,
not what St. Francis had in mind when he dubbed

his body "brother donkey," a dead weight even his
god couldn't shed fast enough. The nature of

sinews is light: in one window, out another. What
we call nightmare is testament to your *creature of a*

different kingdom, dancing for you exotic *sarabandes*;
even the soul stands lead-footed before it.

*Marcel Proust

Lost Forest

A small forest
walking through us
has lost its way.
It can't find the path it was on.
It's been missing for centuries
and it's starting to grow weak
waiting for the search party.
Some of the leaves have raindrops
pinned to them like transparent name tags.
We should find them before we forget who they are.
We should find them before the nametags disappear.
Every evening in the city clocks eat from their troughs
and our shadows lengthen in the street
like dark receipts from a concrete cash register.
As if this life can be returned to the store for another.
But there is no other life. There is barely this one.
We can feel the lost forest inside us closing its eyes.
A sorrow belonging to everyone floats through air
like graffiti without a wall.

A Digression on Hunting

Still, I've never used a gun myself of course or set traps or
lived off the land by living on and from it, eating birds, berries,
or fish taken in season, not even in my wildest dreams of childhood
self-sufficiency when I was Crusoe in the yard and the yard
was not yet lawn and deer and pheasant thought it home, each of us
arrived from somewhere else and not certain exactly of the others
or of standards of behaviour – a ring-necked pheasant, male and
    handsome,
burst into my room one day, scattering glass like shotgun pellets,
and sat stunned in the corner by my bed until I, afraid, refusing
my family's wish (mine too) to eat the bird for Christmas dinner,
    gathered
him up and carried him downstairs to earth again, setting him free;
but I have written a little and so can speak with some authority on
    hunting:
it is, at its best at least, an art of love not violence, a science too,
the work of waiting, of knowledge gained by accident and increments
with, against, across the grain of patience, longing, and fatigue, as well
as by the grace of those who came before and left their love, their lore
behind, an art in which the hunter only sometimes brings proof
of having long since been out at sea, in the bush, or with the muses
on the mountaintops, alone despite the others, searching out the living
traces – dung, a breaching fin, the broken echoes of the dead –
till slowly you become whatever it is you came to take in truth,
now one with the other creatures in their metamorphic passages
where salmon flesh gives rise to bear, caribou to wolf, poets to
    precursors:
still and all, there's little hunting at its best in the several worlds where
I grew up, where at times I've killed and mangled living things myself:
    bugs
and frogs, a wounded bird, the odd book, an imagined enemy or two.

Late Light

For Carole Galloway

Time to paint the sky behind
the boundary spruce: those thoughtful clouds –
misty quilts, smoky blankets, dusted pillows; the rusty
industry of distance, the instant since of dusk.

Meanwhile that row of fusty nutcrackers
standing in for poplars beyond the end of summer.
Lined up at a certain bar that only serves whiskey
to creatures with whiskers. Giving the wind a break,

forever upstaging each other, trying to remember what
they've meant. Marking time until lucent 'witches knickers'
spook their upper branches, feral hares burrowing below.
So the weather of this world supposes you.

The best of the feeder birds have agreed to stay on
for as long as they're needed. Nobody actually lives here
who can't plan to be somewhere else. And by now you can
see your breath. Everything noted for later remains

unsung. Mirrors shiver
your absence. Silence pretends to refuse to have
its say. Empty rooms clear
their throats. O the wonder of our wondering, lighting

pale candles to draw imaginary angel-moths circling
their own questions while we grin again in recognition.
By chance we take our chances, making something of
the choosing, our undoing done in just in time, doing

the best we can despite it. So much of what we have
is so much less than who we have to be. At least
the kitchen clock you finally leave behind at last
gives up, and the love of your life lets go.

Auden's House

The vice-Mayor meets us at the station
in a car meant for children's soccer –
bench seats arranged like pews in the back.
Each one a measured, isolated prayer.

The house is lived in now. Only two rooms
upstairs still marked as his. One the study,
and one the display. My ex-lover keeps
the vice-Mayor talking so I can sit

at the great man's desk, look down
into the garden where they had martinis
on the lawn. (He made a very stiff martini,
said the vice-Mayor, earlier.) The study

seems oddly Canadian, with its wood panelling;
cottage windows. A view to the green hills and the
sound of the highway. The chair is hard, straight-
backed. The desk smooth as paper under my hand.

Auden wrote every day. He loved writing, and this
is what I loved about him when I first started.
It seemed uncomplicated, his relationship to words.
But I was just young. I was uncomplicated.

"Poetry makes nothing happen," said Auden.
I could say it makes nothing good happen.
The choice is always the experience or the poem.
For a while you can pretend otherwise.

But it's really like this – an ex-lover
I've mostly ignored, keeps the vice-Mayor busy
so I can sit at the poet's desk.
Love is just the rough draft for the poem.

Isn't it? Or worse, the idea. The inspiration.
I don't want this to be the same, tired
story of youthful passion fading to middle-aged
apology. I don't want to write poems

with too many questions in them, or with the
bittersweet reflective moment as the geese fly overhead.
But it's already happened. It's always already
happened by the time you vow against it.

The geese don't care that they're a redemptive
symbol. At some point, shouldn't this matter?
"The body is the only truth," said Auden.
But, no, I don't believe that anymore either.

The body is the necessary truth. It's not
the only one.

I think this view is probably still your view,
Wystan. I like your neat rows of paperback
detective fiction. I like your ratty tartan
shopping bag behind glass, and the photo

of you stepping out of the grocery with it
over your arm, full of vegetables.

A Toast to Matthew, after Death

I want to say there was vast injury to more
than me, that all altered; your house gutted

by wind, the doors blown from the hinge. I
want to say that birds began flying, stunned,

into each other, that even the dirt turned
to troubling itself over you. But, in all truth

very little has changed: the phlox has taken
over the cobbled walk, the clouds are directed

by the weather-vane. The old cow leads herself
to the mud now, sloping her head in the small

hope of heeding you again, of feeling the load
of your hand on her. What we had believed

could not live long without us, stirs up flies,
staggers stubbornly through. Here's to you.

Orphic Hymn

It salmons from leagues of leafmulch
         and writhes to the door.
Oak leaf shadow craters its spine range and neck
    as if it walked between being's lit breasts and the screen.
It's got caught, opened in its antlers, the wood-covered 16th century
      book
that works out I am sick.
I hold this up to what I am doing, lying on the divan, haven't pissed
or shit in days, infection's horse's rider lashes back and forth
with his black flag. Two winter stars with dessert plate heads
two months ago were nailed at either edge of my groin.
I've been pensioned a shield of bees
below my chin, under earliest skin, a bridge, a sleeve of industry.
The MRI tech asked if I like country or classical.
The dogwood tree blooms in the full window a rising whine.
The temperature of this nuzzles in like sediment that's already stone.
A knife waits, girlish, down the hill, flipping over, over, small
    fish flash at the bottom of that boat, convinced, the knife, crossing
and uncrossing its legs.

The Scale of Intensity

1) Not felt. With a voice of waves.
   Capitals report flocks of birds low between towers.
   In sensitive individuals, strange cough, homesickness, déjà vu.

2) Detected by adolescents and domestic pets.
   Bananas peel. Grapes deflate. Leaves rustle.

3) Europe wakes. With a voice of whistling seawind.
   Fine china chinks. Staples and safety pins magnetize, inch across
      tables.

4) Pimples bubble beneath skins of paint. In northern hemisphere,
   reports of metallic taste in mouth. Cases of beer open themselves
   in fridge. Changes in viscosity and colour of water. Domestic
   violence.

5) Africa wakes. With a cry of stormbirds. Citrus fruits burst.
   Radio hosts fall silent. Doorbells ring. Vibrations like
      out-of-service
   subways passing. Hair stands on end.

6) Towers sway visibly in skyline. Teeth loosen. Anthropomorphic
      clouds
   reported in southern hemisphere. Branches wave madly.
      Draining water
   stands still then changes vortex direction. Bells ring. Mass
   demonstrations.

7) Strangers attack one another. Tablecloths become reflective.
   Perceptible
   decrease in weight of objects. Amnesia and uncontrollable
   sneezing.
   Cutlery clatters insanely in drawers. China shatters and blends in
   cabinet.

8) Lobsters won't boil. Wild animals stare at one another. Roadkill
   twitches. Hardwood floors moisten. Water doesn't drain.
   Metallic
   objects grind towards New Mexico. Meat flaps on grill.

9) Shadow puppetry reported on Doppler and Accuweather radar.
   Ships
   in harbour rise, rest atop the winedark sea the sea. Systematic
   murder
   of minorities. Cracks in ground. Standing waves loom frozen and
   brown.

10) Hair falls out. Widespread rape and murder of children. Dark
    aurora
    around sun. Unbearable three-tone ringing in ears. Towers snap.
    Roadkill
    resurrects. Religious jewelry ascends from necks.

11) Weightlessness. Feet hover and kick. Towers detach. Oceans
    stand. Universal self-mutilation. Laughter.

12) Eyes closed. Arms outstretched. Ascension at full speed.
    Curvature
    of earth perceptible. Hands clenched. Everywhere white.

after Don Paterson

July

> I hear the wind,
> my dreams, disasters, my own strange name.
> – John Thompson

I.

My mother, ninety-one, howls on my answering machine,
"I want to go home."

Many years ago I saw a man carrying a sleeping child.
I tell my daughter, "That's when I knew I wanted to have you."

Hitch-hiking. No rides. Kerouac's desolation. Useless words.
Rain obscures everything but the yellow line.

Waking to the smell of juniper berries, resin.
Squirrels dropping pinecones on my head.

Swimming in Big Wheeling Creek, thinking
of my cousin who drowned in the Ohio River.

Today I walk in my garden,
worrying about my heart.

II.

Sufficient unto the day. An evil dog.
The devil, running, hides behind blows of wheat.

Sheets on a line, Clorox and sunshine:
now face to face. Unearth me.

Love pads like a cat. The train mumbles by.
I feel old. Atenolol has slowed my heart.

Pottery umbrella stand, bronze cast of a lady's head:
surely someone else is in charge of these things.

When I go to bed, my heart forgets its rhythm.
Neither of my kids is sleeping at home tonight.

III.

An unlocked church. Hillside. A fountain.
You can't look directly at the eclipse.

The decoder ring in the cereal box. Secret formula.
Words tumble out like pills.

Chopping onions, first into lines, then into squares.
I could walk away.

A taste like heavy metal on my tongue. In suspension.
Coins heavy in my pocket. The bridge leads to town.

Know in part. Cobalt blue paint, a starry vault.
I watch my own heartbeat on the monitor.

When I was a child, they lied to me.
What can I put away now?

IV.

Loosestrife, chamomile, hawthorn, juniper.
Pocket full of posey.

My mother in California howls on my answering machine, "Get me
      out of here."
Crows mobbing a broad-tailed bird.

As World War Two was ending, an old man appeared at our door,
    selling laundry soap.
Wringer washer, bluing. Power lines crisscross the sky.

My cousin wiped out on his bike at the end of our alley.
Dead a week later, he still had the grit ground into his hand.

The sea is not far from here.
I seldom go to look at it.

My wife, my love,
I'm thinking of you.

V.

A week of rain in fits and starts. Dried seeds shaken in a coffee can.
Colours of wet leaves on sidewalks. Kids' raincoats.

I have seen the silences of children. Moss green
kneesocks and tartan skirts. Ochre of roasted rice in *genmaicha*.

Surely some revelation, according to thy word.
Arouse the mind without fixing it anywhere.

The formalized emotion of Japanese poetry. My mother came in early
to light the heater in my room. I wrote: "Waking hungover.

Sunday morning. Bird singing.
Somewhere in the rain."

VI.

All perils and dangers of this night. The stone that presses,
the cat that sucks, the mare that tramples.

My heart. The hour of the fly. A Philco radio
with a green plastic dial. A rock collection. Lighten us.

Kitchen linoleum. Frost. Milk bottles frozen on the doorstep,
wearing their lids like hats. My cousin has been dead forty-two years.

Now lettest thou thy servant depart in peace
to find the next thing, and the next thing after.

VII.

To bind to myself a joy.
The habit of remembering.

My mother can't remember our last conversation. She can't
remember
the beginning of the conversation we're having right now.

Alone all night in Strathcona Park,
I prayed to the Buddha in the woods with the bears.

We're the names we give things.
We're a closed hand.

John Thompson's chopping block. Mine's
split into three pieces from being washed in hot water.

My kids come to me when they need slivers removed.
I don't want to write anymore today.

VIII.

Death is not a white owl. Chaos.
Spikes to 240 beats per minute.

Heart monitor. No light, but rather
fibrillation visible.

Debris driven out from the nuclear blast. Gale force winds,
waves of howling RADs. Then

is our faith. Nothing but this: take one breath
and the next breath after. In vain.

We long for an end to pain,
not for an end to what perceives the pain.

Nothing is metaphor. Disconnect
the electrodes. A non-event.

IX.

In the last weeks of his life my uncle Will Brown
watched a spider build a web.

Don't touch me, I have not yet. Fragile as a new butterfly.
An ant's forefoot shall save you.

My daughter Elizabeth has grown tall. She irons her hair.
I miss the years when she was little.

Maybe it's a matter of taking care. The long northern twilight,
smokey peat fires. Church bells. Nunc Dimittis.

Look for me tomorrow,
I won't be anywhere.

The monk laughs at the same tired goldfish. Dying,
my friend Joyce wrote: Situation hopeless but not serious.

x.

A kid my daughter knows got stoned and wrote all over herself:
shoe labeled "shoe," knee labeled "knee," head labeled "head."

I drift my car down the winding roads from Caulfeild Village.
My roses and lavender, my rosemary and thyme, under the high sun.

This yellow afternoon is full and round as the Island stadium.
Elizabeth sleeps in the basement.

I'm thinking of the Ohio River, deviled crabs and the bang
of the screendoor, a little girl twirling her baton, sweat on her lip.

Tonight I will broil chicken with honey, lemon, and pepper.
The house will tick, cooling. The doorspring churr of the nighthawks.

How long can I link these things, one to another? At the foot
of my street, the sea casts runes with itself and remembers.

xi.

Tiny pellets of shot in pan-fried squirrel.
The day divided by butterscotch wafers.

This shaking. What falls away.
I haven't been drunk in twenty years.

Things I was going to do later: learn to fly an airplane,
live in a penthouse overlooking Manhattan, write a great book, marry
    a princess.

As the day cools, I will walk across the suspension bridge,
read *Sports Illustrated* in the Ohio County Public Library.

I dreamed of a post
that refused to be put to any use whatsoever.

Sing a new song, for this clear evening
is waiting where you have misplaced it.

XII.

Though I speak with tongues, chopping my words
on a black-and-white monitor,

can my mother remember her vegetable garden
that I remember from '47?

I wake to a heart rate of fifty beats per minute.
I throw away the Atenolol.

My dancing daughter, my sleeping daughter,
my wife in the bathtub, running water,

rain and pinecones fall on my table.
The strange old man is up the mountain.

Sleeping with the River

All that winter as the rains arrived,
sometimes as nobody's footsteps,
sometimes as ack-ack, sometimes
hard bits of Braille flung at the house,
the mailbox, the woodshed, at the car parked
in the driveway, at all that is solid, all
that winter leaving the window open to its
pizzicati, hearing them accelerate and blend and
drown in the river's big
ambiguous chorus, all that winter being
swept asleep thinking river is only rain
that has its act together, song that has never
passed through speech, unschooled,
other-than-us, thinking
this must be the voice of what-is as it
seizes the theme, pours its empty opera,
pumps out its bass line of sea-suck and blues.

Odds and Ends

An evil swamp meadow, burnt and sawed.
Invisibly small lives hum and rummage
in fearful humidity. Among the stumps
lean six pine saplings, the bare slender trunks
tipped with cone-shaped tufts of needled twigs:
greenery arrowheads. What made these arrow-trees
fall here notch first and sink their feathers
under the lava flow of golden weed –
what, beyond some whim and power of nature
and ideal of the painter, inexpressible in words?

I was glad as always to leave the museum
and regain the town and again be living
in a picture, restored to our nature as pilgrims
for the ideal law. But when the walk did not turn
and open on the sea, as map misreading had told me,
my eyes settled on a fallen rhododendron flower.
Its petals, intact and perfect, were in fact
not petals but five rays of a single disc,
shadowy rose, with a circular hole at center.
It was a skirt for a dead Romantic waist:
the upturned, golden, hammer-headed pistil
had fit there, with its garden of ten stamens waving
ovular flecks, and these remained above
on their bush withering, while the shed pink dirndl
was put away in the grass.

                        O clothes she wore
and we put them away for her to wear again
someday, and today they lie there still.

Chardin's Rabbit

Lilac bough limp with rain
hanging across the fence, in the arc
of Chardin's rabbit (vertical, yet falling,
tethered to a leather looped from one stiffened leg
to a thick beam in the ceiling, its shiny eye like a seed
of oil. An inverted crucifixion framed by an oval
of darkness, the rabbit's head resting
on the edge of a worn and battered butcher's block.
Pigment painstakingly built up grey over mauve,
bristled, blood-stained ears pointed, alert
at the moment of death). I imagine the lilacs,
clusters of dampened light, will spring back
buoyant when morning comes climbing
up the white fence pickets. I step across
interlocking brick, shake the bush –
no dead rabbit masterpiece – rather,
simple woody boughs, various wet leaves,
deepening shades of green, bundles of mauve.
Cut one. Shake it. Vase it under carnal light.
Blossoms lift, living room fills with lilac desire.
Hopeful, I meet you with smile
and clean skin, the sun arrives for our kiss
across the frame of your bicycle. A good kiss,
brave meeting of lips in the middle of the street.
I look up to you. Not because you are tall (and you are tall),
but rather because our eyes lock and yours water gold,
and it isn't a reflection of sun or the light changing
across your face, it's the weight of those
gold-earth eyes that takes me by the throat.
A kiss through opening sky.
Sun warmed us both. I saw the interplay
of grace and sadness on your face

when you told me about your wife.
Between us was the brilliant frame
of your bicycle, its spinning spoke, the sincere wedge
of your voice. Above us, the oil-black cloud of the lie.

Playground Incident

This is the swing that snapped,
hurling the boy. Limp rubber, chain
coiled in mud.
Blossoms of blood
bear witness: the boy was flung,
fussed over, whisked away,
he and his twisted wrist, in the declining day.

Here, the wake of that panicked evacuation:
hanged seat and soil askew;
one mitt cast off before the breaking
of the fall; the shadows voices leave;
fallen leaves imprinted with alarm.

Doctors wrested the wrist straight.
They've seen worse; the boy will live.

Rust winds like vines around the pole,
the hollow socket where the chain sprang loose.
Flakes of paint, once livid,
cling to the crater's lip
and the sun slips
and early raccoons snuffle, prod the mitt.

One day he will sit down in a dim office,
having accepted his first promotion.
One rung of light penetrates the blinds.
He stares at pallid stacks of files,
time whiled and tasks fulfilled.

A lurching is in his belly,
A widening to and fro there in his gut.
His temples pound and are rent with it.

Later tonight there will be rain;
mud will overwhelm the red drops.
Steadily the mitt's wool will decay,
sodden and trodden under other boys' feet.
All evidence will be ground away,
the swing fixed, the chain complete.

The Dream World

Shake up envy. Shake up
the impulse toward acquisition –
it batters you nightly, a moth at a bulb.
Shake up the trope of the moth at a bulb:

words take shape in fresh combination,
cheerleaders on court at halftime. A girl tossed
skyward, bent at the waist, a check mark
against a ballot's blank box. Vote for the moment,

vote for atonement, for taking a long walk alone
through the forest. Morning is raising
its snapping white flag. You exit the alders, hands
in the air, and wake: your final surrender.

To float, to drown, to close up, to open – a throat

where the great artery rises and crosses, coming so close
to the larynx, the lynx in larynx, the animal voice
in its first low growl –

Over the kitchen table, night, after lamp is lit, voices
of the grandmother and grandfather lifting into the low beams
of the small old house, the pitch rough –

Under the low roof in the attic above we can hear them
after we stop giggling. Together we shut out
the fear of the dark. The black so black,
nights with no moon. The beds so deep we drift
down to sleep. Into feathers and flannel –

their sounds lifting and falling,
pitched low, a mixture of stove black and coal tar,
hardwood and well water, its taste startling
cold, up out of the ground. The sounds
coming into us – into me. The green painted table,
curved chair backs, the brown teapot, cracked and porous –
Still there – grandfather's axe, biting
into the root of the apple tree blown over by wind: *There's life in it yet.*
Haul it back up. The oxen, the ropes, the straining – august apples,
Yellow Transparents – the best ones, worth saving.

The things that enter you before you know you're
breathing in – the things that grab hold of the voice box,
climb up into the throat – Sound of the pig squeal
muffled, shut out, morning of the pig death, the cauldron
prepared, great vat of scalding water, the kids all sent down the hill
to play by the shore – The scream, the blood – Was there a shot?
Heard or imagined, which is worse –

The sound of crab apples running down the chute to the pig's trough –
only yesterday – and milk, a bucket of milk and slop for the hungry,
vociferous sow – clean sided, white and pink, bright eyed,
sweet. Down by the river shore, the dragonfly with its darning needle –
It will come and sew up your mouth – lighting on the river rocks,
landing on some kid's arm. The river water soft – half fresh,
half salt – It tastes so good in your mouth. Cadence coming with the
    tide,
turning tongue of the tidal river lifting the small soft fragments of rock,
each piece worn, flat – tiny pieces stuck to the soles of your feet. Lap
of the arriving water pressing into the shore, the river's edge graduated,
    sheltered –
its language erasing now, the sounds civilized, modulated –
Language tied to the land – sound of the lawn mower – old sharp
scrape of the whetstone waiting in its can of rusty water
to edge and hone the scythe – translated, embedded,
repeated, remembered, half lost – The crab apples
all run over the ground. Worms in them, sow bugs
in the fence posts, thousands of shingle flies.

The slain pig, white carcass stretched from a rafter
in the dim, forbidden barn –

To float, to drown, to open, to close up – a heart:
arch of the aorta, rounded over the valentine, its upper border
an inch below the top of the breast bone –

                              In the woodshed –
a girl picks up the sharpened hatchet, selects the best piece of pine,
(no knots) places it on the block: one, two – she is making a boat:
pointed bow, straight stern. Her grandfather will growl if he sees her
in here – but he knows. All the kids do it – she works in secret:
pieces fit together, a cabin, a bridge. Shingle nails line the deck
to make a railing defined by string. She cannot get

enough string. The boat is beautiful. After dinner she takes it
to the river shore. This is the summer of Uncle Jack – the girl is eleven.

When she is eighteen, she visits him – and Aunt Peggy, most beautiful
of the aunts – in Montreal. She goes to a concert in a slender dress, he
buys her a gardenia, a record – Dinu Lipatti playing Mozart. He says
he wants to be a writer, that the old people in Sable River are important –
that they have changed his life. She wants to fall to her knees when she
    sees him.
She wants to press her forehead into the door frame and breathe him in.

The summer she is eleven, he takes her to Johnson's Pond Beach
and pitches golf balls into the sand. She follows him down the beach –
he flashes his smile at her. She runs away when she sees him
drinking beer with the other uncles at the open trunk of the car –

All that is left is a photograph: Jack in his air force uniform – light
grey wool, hair slicked back. The smile. The writer in her. *He drank* –

Heart squeezed – barbed wire on the top strand of the fence,
cows in the pasture, alder switch flicking their sides to make them run.

High tide – full river, dark brown water from the Tom Tigney
flowing down. Swimming holes. Kids swinging on the rope, upriver,
tied to the maple tree. Uncle Jack with his camera. Seeing
from the outside – making her beautiful. Jack
on the swinging bridge, kissing someone else –

To close up, to open – the piano – heart soaring. You can feel
a pulse beating there, just where the clavicle (collar bone)
articulates with the sternum, that same little hollow. Smell
of the practice rooms. Wood and varnish. Felts on the hammers.
Precision. Bach, Scarlatti. Running scales. Heart breaking –

every piano lesson a mission – Breath in the line,
perfect rendition. Never – never, never. A sonata by
Scarlatti: sent to Spain to compose for Isabella, finds
his form. Two pages: diptych. Mirror. Listen – reverse
symmetry. Here, the theme, modulated tonic to dominant:
page two, dominant back to tonic. A closed world – she can
live there. Love knots form harmonic clusters – melodic line, driven
into the page. Shoulders knot in the practice room. A prelude
by Bach unbends the line. Care, care, in every chromatic interval –
Glenn Gould will take the whole tissue, render it perfect – Until then,
her girl's heart believes – will strike each note into the listener's
yearning heart. Will play in the basement room of the little house on
Zwicker Ave, in Liverpool, for her mother's closest friends. Music,
    music –
live – in the room. The damp air, the red and blue tile floor, the
Heintzman upright. One day, one day – she will take the stage,
drown in the Steinway grand, its gold interior. Burn, inside out –
for the sound, transmission of sound –

The Blanket

The label reads: 100% UNDETERMINED FIBRES.
Like everything kept in the upstairs closet, wedged in
Among the tilting mismatched strata of our pasts combined,
It's of unknown provenance, its value ripe for dispute.

Eerily weightless, it will not lie flat, makes you imagine
The rounds and pockets hide sloughed pajamas,
Ambulant pillows, balled-up animals or some other body lost in sleep.
Its colour resolves, on staring, into a purplish blue-grey,

Like a pointillist rendering of a soiled pigeon on a dull day.
In short, a blanket of nothing so much as vulcanized lint
Bought from (and possibly made of) Canadian Tire,
Forged when a nation's aspirations rested on miracle fibres,

A vestige made of tail-ends, waste, god knows what else.
Lie under it, and the heat that builds to something scorching
Is all your own. What you walk around, giving off all day is
Thrown back, until you're swamped, broiled hot as shame.

But if I'm tired, I don't care. I pull it down and over me.
And somewhere in sleep's plush furnace the mind
Pulls strands, indiscriminate, the weave of the day
Is laced with the shimmer of limitless unknowing:

The sleep that blanket brings is unnatural and deep.
Sometimes I've left it out, and you've succumbed.
I see it on the bed, arched in a curve borrowed
From your spine. As if it, too, expected to rise and go.

The Great Leap Forward

*

and none and none and none and none and un-

*

zip, a light before light, quickening, like children

*

of early enzymes feasting, each of each, protean
seas gone glacier, gathering footprints, thread, skin

*

for collection at the Exhibit of Humans, a mountain
casting a mould from a city of walls and curs, women
at wash with basins of ashen water and no reflection

*

to recognize their own husbands in a crowded pavilion
of charlatans, quack doctors, snake-oil salesmen
shilling goat glands for impotence, a foolproof gin,
horse semen brandy, and on the buckboard, a Christian
with hurdy-gurdy accompaniment hawking salvation

*

in the antebellum lands, where black winds separate kin
from kin, and the people of the plains hear the coming din
of cattle crossing the continent forty days before it even
begins, and leaded tins of fruits and vegetables poison
Franklin and his men, leaving them delirious and rotten
in the head, composed of thoughts and faith in a northern
passage from ocean to ocean that consumes them like vermin
in the clutch of an owl, picked to pieces, or else frozen

*

in the mind like that line from Keats we failed to learn,
heard melodies are sweet, unheard sweeter, so play on
into the cool afternoon of touching under tables, linen
hung on the line, saxifrage, stonecrop, phlox and gentian,
common-touch-me-not, the meadow beyond our garden
gate opening into bittersweet, death camas, fool's onion,
and again farewell-to-spring arrives in the parched season
of brittle grass, titian leaves, auburn and tawny crimson
infecting the edge of things, as dusk draws from dawn
to envelope us in dark arms like hope or lust, wintergreen,
the flowering weeds we kneel in without naming one
or all or none, for that is a kind of love we call possession
and have abandoned, *Dominus vobiscum,* a woman, a man

A-frame

Hello, I announce, though this isn't quite right and I know it.
I'm in someone's backyard and don't wish to be taken
to say they're in mine: mortgaged and pinned at this ecotone's edge
ten minutes walk by the course of a trail. The word

is just a frame of language I enter the scene through. Upstrung
ridgepole: hinge to a mud-worn tarpaulin pinned open at sixty
degrees to the earth. Spruceboughs leant and packed with moss
against the blue plastic tent to make it not one. The ground

is frozen now. A split white bale of fibreglass
betrayed the shelter, drew me off the path:
white patch inside the leafless trees
before first snowfall – a plan abandoned,

left for squirrels to make
a fitful winter of, they can't resist. *Hello?*
I say again. The moss-lined bed, dull
shimmer of the zippered nylon bag a snarl

of coming from and going to. Outside,
the forest deepens, leans upon itself so every
branch and trunk becomes a doorway.

I hand myself through passages
unstopping till the evening
air gives way to snow –

once more,
Hello.

If it was the sea we heard

Penelope's Song

Whose sea?

The sun up this early and how.

Going forth from the knees to a truant happiness.

Will be finished in one tall order, they assured us, pecking wives on cheeks, rubbing the curly heads of children.

The rustle of wind through sheep shit and sand flies. The usural torpidity of the morning and its general direction of decay.

A density in their eyes offered up the shy event of our reckoning to a pampered heart.

They took oars to water as an end to privileges of place and turned heels to breaker with morning sun upon the rosined water, their bodies hip deep in swelling surf.

Through the surf's ebb and draw, they moved the stalwart ship.

Every utterance we gave was the true one.

They set sail to wind, canvas snapping.

As they moved into the furthest wave with its back upon the buried reef, water up from sudden depths beyond the shifting shoals, our hands tired.

We turned our backs upon the ocean roar.

These men over the ocean's small but growing depths, I remember.

Of doubt, soiled ghosts?

Theirs the calm of raging waters, fettered by borders of acceptable blame.

The end I see in this old order dismantled nightly, step for step ahead, to an end greeded by sleep.

Much doesn't care for my place in this story of unlikely return.

A tearmoist body a man could wreck against.

Night ravels me.

On King George's Crowning

On King George's crowning, the interviewee
said they all got sweets and little goodies, and when
they come by boat, some come as stowaways. Once

they collect money for this woman's fare. Others
come, a fiver tight in their pockets, like my grandfather
when he escaped from the belly of the crown and never

spoke of it again. Others not bring overcoat –
no one told them how air moves vampires through
bone, erases memory matter. Some dress in suits

tropical style, as the ship moved its shaky
hand over the old surface of the sea. They arrive,
say 'I born Jamaican, I die Jamaican,' take a bite

of the sweet, hand to mouth, take the test
of motherland's history – bitter – replied, when asked if
they spoke the Queen's English; Enoch Powell's rivers

of blood forming a new oxygen, scarlet-marked
as they sliced through London fog; iris recording
life, how it is: Houses of Parliament, Big Ben

in the grey dank; a room, a galvanized tub to wash, emerge
baptized; the city soot, a new glove for the body; the signs
reading no Irish or blacks or dogs, not wanted but

take your money, just the same. Some, some,
carry hope like luggage, others not so sure-footed, others
not so childlike in believing all what this mother have to say.

Some bring formal names, leave pet ones behind,
whisper night bougainvillaea. How this country
cold, cold, cold through and through and no tea hot

enough to warm you, or hand friendly enough to pry
open the dark days, bring morning brightness. Some come,
stay, patience worn thin like paper, hearts

tough as old bread, and letters back home with every
copper earned from the Double Decker, brow wipe
of the sick, hammer of nail into two by four – if they

let you, if you not too dark for their liking.
Some, some, come long way, did bite
of the sweet. Motherless mother's milk.

Ol' Englan'
cryin' crocodile tear
for her lost chil'ren.

I Don't Remember Telling the Stepsons

But when we drive down Gondola Drive,
My father's street in Orlando, while
I am trying to bend memory, shirts, yearning,
Stray conversations and these boys
Into something that looks like, to the
Untrained eye, anyway, *a family*
They say This is where you jumped
Off the roof bleeding and This is the yard
Where you left your father for dead and
Here's where you sped with Todd Gele.
You made out with him over there.
We can't believe you spray painted
that guy's entire yellow Torino pink.

My new husband says, as we crawl
Down Orange Blossom Trail
(That's the Chi-chi's where you
Worked where everyone did cocaine)
Why can't your schoolwork be this
Thorough, guys? And I keep saying
This is all changed and I do not remember
Telling you any of these things.
I do not recall remembering the car,
The kiss, the father left for dead, that
Motorcycle, my Orlando heart.

In those days I was thinking now,
Not *I'll marry a man with two boys*
A three for one special and raise them.
Then it was jackpot, fry chicken, syllables of
Ruin, it was possibly porn star baby
With shades of Actress, Saudi prince,

Dulcinea, Quiana, Candies and surf
Culture – I could see the sun rise on one
Beach and set over the other. This made
The world seem endless and me possible.
Did you ever get in trouble for anything?
The boys ask and the husband says
Turn here? Tell me now or else.

Song for the Call of the Richardson's Ground Squirrel Whose Call is a Song for the Cry of the Short-Eared Owlet (They May One Day Meet for Dinner)

In the cow pasture across the road, it may simply be
a trick of the light, an eyelash trapping the dusk.
They seem there, and there, and there and then gone.
Prairie mirages. But the call is unmistakable –
syncope of blue sky, fear, and the Swainson's Hawk's
lethal dive. Jazz interruptions in a calm Saskatchewan evening.
Nothing anyone can say is more humourless. Imagine
three cats in a bag. High-pitched, furry whoopee
cushions, a litany of helium balloons wheezing
out their last. Jack-knives puncturing the tires
on the bastard neighbour's unmufflered Datsun.
It's alarming enough to make you want to run home
and count the kids. Who knows? With such fleet, thieves' hands
perhaps they're only lamenting their lack of pockets
before ducking back into invisible kingdoms;
what choruses and sudden confusions, casualties,
among the families in those dark territories.
When you live for so long beneath the horizon
there must only be a language of weeping.
Listen as they peer partially, cautiously
back into the sunset world.

Sweetness

i

He bends over rows,
eases pink, thin-skinned tubers free
of root systems, sandy loam,
to *thunk* in plastic buckets.

Stink beetles, 'hoppers, and big green caterpillars
skittle over spilled soil
whose darkness the hard sun pales.

Bees light at waters puddled
where irrigation seams drip,
they suck at man-high sunflowers.

ii

His gaze wanders in the room,
a tea-house made of cowboy lumber,
board fit to board along the contour of the warp
in a harmony of imperfections,

slips through redwood knots to the
storming range behind.

– Can't stay inside. My eye follows the line
of the room. My eye
swivels back on itself.

She speaks to a third, for him to hear:

Perfectionists: they're not easy to get along with,
even when they're feeling good.

A duet of difference, he thinks:

– She has bones like a bird's. She
knows the names of things.
She grows lettuce and arugula in the shaded hoops.

– My husband has a lot of anger.
But he's a visionary, he sees how things will be.
Those're just stakes now, but that's where

the Japanese bath will be...
He goes stir-crazy out working in the heat
with no one to talk to.

– Vision is the coldest sense, the most distant,
and I'm not worth any love today.

Now to him alone:

– But you see *out* with your eyes!
– That's nice of you to say.

Once he drove up the road to the farm,
streamers of wild bees flung behind the truck.

iii
After work, after lunch, restful in the shade
of out-buildings, some conversation:

– The sweetest of sweets is alcohol.
If you want to digest the past, the painful past,
stay away from the sweet things.

He has a root beer float,
zinc on his nose. Chickens want feeding:

– Those hives were fierce.
I killed the queen, put a gentler one in her place.
And they all calmed down.

Sprinkler chirrs and repeats, greening a
square of clover. One hundred five degrees. She says:

– They all calmed down after that.

Jeremiah Scrounges Rest

J walks through highway shrubbery, muttering ballyhoo reels in a rip-torn baritone. Over top the puddles and paddies, the dank skunk cabbage and root-rotted cone pines, bits of broken burg waft up to trickle his nose. J knows what it is. Was. Brick falls over too, just ask the three pigs. Through haze, must, and should, J spies a new development: a yard! And a bone-brained retriever walking his dog. J hawks on his heel and rubs a cranky corn. Ahoy! The man wheels, and J pumps a cracked fist into a low-hanging ash branch. The dog browfs friendlily. Have you seen the Tent of Meeting? Don't-want-any-trouble tells him the nothing he knows. Nobody here but us and chickens. J clucks. Splat on the old milltown, now two-lane close enough to the Pitt to croon for communing commuters. Burg transmutes to burb. At least there's the lawn, freshly mowed, thistles and crabgrass chemo'ed to a luminescent greed. Who could ask for a better bed? J hefts his hunker-down. Man says Listen. J says Hey. Man looks elsewhere, browfer still bounding. Settle down there. One night's hospitality won't harm your well-worn get-ahead.

Squash Rackets

For they know us by our grip and the swordsmanship
of our swing. For they are chrome lariats
always bellowing, "here I come to save the day!"
For they love, whenever possible, the crosscourt smash
and channel our inner thug for that grunting drive.
Let us praise the harum-scarum rallies
that sound and re-sound like thank-offerings to the walls.
Let us praise the unretrievables that die in back corners.
Now a drop, now a short shot, and now a low
second bounce caught by the lip and tipped to the T-line.
For they can throw their voice into any part of the room.
For they are patient with eked-out backhands, iffy returns, serves
 skied high,
forehand boasts that are all wallop and no wattage.
For they live for deadly wrap-arounds,
balls knuckling down the side wall into the nick,
fast roll-outs. A pox on the slow! Let us not deal in mincing steps.
Let us lunge and stretch in the crouch-and-pounce footwork,
digging out those hard-to-get backwall shots.
Oh, that moment before the quick kill, the scything slice,
the short angle aimed to hit low.
For life, from their point of view, is like a camera, handheld and
 thrust into the tumult.
For they dread the instant the squeaks of our shoes move
from wolf whistle to SOS.
For they are the boo that causes a straight drive's dead run
to turn tail, double back along the rail.
For they dock the head off anything uppity, tall-poppied,
floating away on its own pretentiousness,
and thus strike a blow for authenticity.
For their ricochets crack like a nail gun snapping metal sheets into
 place.

For the din, getting to speed, soon turns the court cavernous and
   warm
with the saline, sweat-pungency of rock.
For when they mouth off they brag *belted* and *poleaxed, hammered* and
   bashed.
For they always ready for what follows.
For your thumb should sit on the handle like you've dropped
the safety catch and are about squeeze off a clip.
For a winning serve is a baffled forensics that follows the bullet as it
   enters
and cleanly exits the whole of the imagination.
For they steal the show with boasts that whiz past the line of senses,
leaving you lightheaded with revs per thought.
For they are always punching loudness into the front wall,
bearing out your effort, mark it verbatim.
For when we miss, they go whoosh as they filter the air through their
   gills.
For they won't laugh at the crosscourt kill where you throw down the
   gauntlet
only to backpedal a bone-shaking run into the side wall.
For they know there is nowhere to go but round.
For they help the game identify itself with each noise *Walaang!*
   Walaang!
as if screams were being ripped from the air.
For they are quid pro quo bats,
and remind you that hitting the ball fast on top of a bounce
finds the shortest distance between two points.
For they let fly comebacks that flatter those bright enough to follow
   along.
For we lug them into a game like buckets sloshing with momentum.
For they can take a galloping rally and bring it down to heel.
For they catch the scent of direction and pull our arm after it.
For they are always spotting something up-range,
chasing the acrobounding prey until it's end-stopped by fatigue

and mid-jink they spoon that ounce of heart
– small, hot, beating in bird-panic – into our hand.
For they are cognoscenti of the picked-off drop,
thought-balloons that think only one thought: sweet spot.
Or tools for what the real world lacks: a lovely, long,
levitational lob with the uncorked
reverb still ringing. You can read between the lines.
After all, the balls leave their spoor everwhere, dark c-shaped
   stutterings on whiteness,
etched echos of old volleys, and below them
us, breathless, hands on our knees, staring at the floor.

Morning after

A few hours of uncertainty by the ocean,
that's all. A blueberry seed rolling in the bowl
of an afternoon. But in a world where this summer
is allowed its momentum, I answer questions:
Your father? We laughed a lot. He had these eyes.
He knew I was leaving. Before you came along
I wondered what kept me so long, pushed my knee
against his under every table. There I was –
top floor of that old yellow house and summer
gone without me – when you burst in
through the latex. Not a care for our plans.
You always were stubborn, little blue.
I moved clear across the country for you.
Bought winter boots and sold the van with no heat.
There's not a lot can stand in your way, remember that.

I walked to the ocean, bottle in my pocket,
and lay in the matted Crowberry. Four flat pills,
to be taken twelve hours apart. I let the wind
blow my hair into knots. The water was thick with colour.
The sun·had made fat blueberries of the summer. The hours
went by one at a time and I spent them as something small
held in the world that would have me. It took most of a day
to swallow the first two. I stayed up late to take the others.
I was lucky: No pain, no nausea, no cramping.
It's not as if I were pregnant. Only two small things
inside me, cancelling each other out. A summer
of suddenly unrelated events falling off a thread like glass beads.
Then I turned to what was left – the van with no heat,
the long highway home, that seedpod of the unhappened
rattling all the way.

Gentlemen of Nerve

I have become my neighbour or the author or the man
I saw in the photo, when I was thirteen; I've slipped in
To his life, the one where you get to be the has-been

Movie writer; get to be the fellow who adores his wife;
The forty-year-old who walks slowly down boulevards
In springtime, thinking of nothing much, sidling along

With a mumble, instead of a song, in his punctured heart;
Now I know what they were doing when they were
Doing it; not exactly, for that was their lot, then; but well

Enough to hum the approximate ontology they unknit.
I have slipped in to the opening along their side,
Entered the weave of their nearby manhood, to coincide

With the shyness of a gentle soul who holds out
For some other day, some boon, a grand foretold
Coming in to confidence (and confidences); a Chump

At Oxford in a silk-lined coat who'd jump a fence
To avoid a bullying leaf or an unkind glance; a gentleman
Gentled by nothing so much as having sort of grown old

Without having ever advanced, in terms of career,
In terms of science, beyond the fields of expectant fear
That the sweet girl who holds him tight might evaporate

And all his books, thoughts and friends will disappear
Like stars, which look quite risky in the sky. So if
I am this guy, where is he now, past having had his own

Slippage moment, when he came into his three-piece Geist?
He might have driven far, stopped at the coast, for a well-
Earned cigar, maestro of leaning knowingly into a sea breeze;

For, the exact moment I turned forty and had insight into *him*
He was set free, to flow or saunter at unidentified ease, no
Longer a person observed or wondered at, but a ghostly skim

Of atoms, then other particles wafting to some inexact home,
As a genie exceeds the prison house of his wishes, to fly late
But gladly beyond the bottle's stoppered rim; so now I hesitate,

Poised, a diver on the doorframe of my impressionable bungalow,
My blissful villa, my flat, my porch, my mansion, my estate –
Until some kid spies me out as curious, unimaginably aged, so

When their grey stubble hits the marker they'll zap to my face,
Slip in to my statehood, reassemble a mixed-blessings-self or two,
While, sweet as rain after drought, I dance out and over as I go.

Encyclopedia of Grass

Here in the window of grass back
And forth, visual grammar up and
Down, omni-poetics, hymn of bees

Within the whorls of milkweed resting
On the white tips of the root system
The prairie fire blew across not quite

Telepathic because it had something to do
with the communication between root hairs
something to do with the negative space of

prairie dog burrows heedless of prairie chickens,
once caught this would go on for miles
once caught, this transferred underground

past the missile silos, a sore throat, a split
thumb, a weapon in the middle of all that land.
Grasshopper tea for supper, empty space

A desert – save for the grass holding down the top soil
the sun was saying something, was singing something,
was demanding something: give me your tongue,

give me your day. I don't want your excuses, your
indeterminations, your missteps. Give me your big dream
The grass studied the word. The grass worried the definitions

stood by the blade
of the phrases: sod bunk
sod dreams, sod stew

cut windows in the sod
sew windows in the sod
freeze windows in the sod

grass seed
contortions of grass
a diorama of grass

the grass museo
the cinema of grass
grass gesture, grass joy

grass kinesis grass
pantomime only
the voice of grass is absent

grass a silent movie without the
disruption of a tree, of anything
taller the grass, arrested grass

bliss in the close whispering
of grass seven feet underground
cry for the long gone winter

the thrill cavalier spread
the musketeer repetition
found somewhere in the morning.

The graft that shapes time, the splint that makes
history the weft that determines what is seen looking
back, talking back, moving backwards, diving in.

Shrove Tuesday

Either Sunday or Monday, it doesn't matter,
Both days were glorious, I was thinking about the structure
Of praise; or, rather, its style – how essential it is
Not to reach for words. I don't know what

Happened to that thought. The bay was blue
With the sky. A broad band of another
Blue followed the shoreline like milk in a glass bowl
Wanting to curdle. There was no wind.

The sun had warmth. The earth held firm
Under stiffening snow. Can I say that I prayed
Without ceasing, cutting a trail in the forest
Above, burning the shed that used to be

A chicken coop? The dog was with me,
Faithful in fatigue, joyous whenever
I might stop. At night I drank beer
In the house of hemlock and pine

We are building before sleep. Tuesday
Was not the same when I returned
To the world I had made. I was expected
To render account. Many people are

Unhappy. It seems I did not
Satisfy. At the tip of my middle finger,
Buried within the calloused swirl, there's now something sore
I can't get out.

POEM NOTES & COMMENTARIES

Maleea Acker, "The Reflecting Pool"

"The Reflecting Pool" was a small pool located on the top of Mount Helmcken, in Metchosin, on Vancouver Island. The mountain was topped by wide meadows of glacier-smoothed rock and thick moss. The pool was in a small patch of fir and Manzanita. A ridge provided views over the entire south island. About a year after the poem was written, a subdivision of luxury homes was built in place of everything it describes.

James Arthur, "Americans"

During the summer of 2002, when I was 27 years old, I spent a few months living in and around Rome. Like so many other young men who have travelled through Italy, writing poems, I was pining away for a married woman. Shortly after my return to North America, I wrote this poem. At the time, I never doubted that I was writing the poem for the woman – but now, when I reread "Americans," I feel that the poem is introspective. I think that I was trying to understand who I was, in that place, surrounded by so much evidence of history, separated from the environment that I knew.

Margaret Avison, "Hag-Ridden"

"Hag-Ridden" was written in Margaret's eighty-eighth year when she was well acquainted with the need to use a cane on her daily walks out under the "mysterious (some days dazzling) sky..."

Ken Babstock, "Hunter Deary and Hospital Wing"

I'd like to think I had lullabies, murder ballads, antibiotic-resistant bacterium, threatened socialized health care, poisoned water tables, and gene therapy in mind when I started the poem, but it was Hunter Deary herself who appeared, in the way fiction writers are heard to talk of their characters; like they'd stepped out of the shadows whole, historicized, speaking like no one but themselves. She's equal parts Cassandra, Rachel Carson, and Flannery O'Connor heroine, plus maybe the person who tended the pumpkin patch Coetzee's Michael K. fed at. And she once knew someone called Hospital Wing. So. The poem is a degraded, or infected, or polluted ballad. It feels like it should go one longer; which is how we think of ourselves, isn't it?

John Wall Barger, "Weather"

I was living with a girl in a dilapidated farmhouse in New Germany, Nova Scotia, with a wood stove, a record player, an old Scrabble game, and some gorgeous decrepit editions of books about tornados, earthquakes, and the flora and fauna of the Maritimes. One marvellous book – called *The Weather*, with chapters like "The Face of the Sky," and "From the Four Winds" – had water-stained black-and-white photos of, for instance, cows beside a tree, labelled "Cumulonimbus in distance, with stratocumulus sheet near zenith." I woke up early each day and walked, bewildered, through the birches with my dog, and wrote all morning in a little room lined with maps. At night, as we played Scrabble, June bugs and moths tapped at the window. When it was time to move back to Halifax, we went our separate ways.

Brian Bartlett, "Dear Georgie"

"Dear Georgie" is one of about a dozen found-reconstructed poems I've written in the past few years, though "written" may be a misleading term here. These poems rely upon the words and phrasings of others, adding nothing though liberally abbreviating some sentences and freely re-arranging their order. The original sources include newspapers, travel books, a school reader, a diary, and, in this case, a great uncle's letters. A handful of sentences might be chosen from hundreds of pages. These poems might be compared to collages or quilting. I found writing them a fascinating experience in trying to hear and celebrate the voices of others, while the degree of creating new voices varied from poem to poem. The poems acknowledge a statement by Don Domanski: "Each of us stands on the shoulders of thousands of men and women who have gone on before us. It isn't just one hand holding the poem or moving across the keyboard."

John Barton, "One Bedroom Apartment"

"One Bedroom Apartment" is part lark, part cri-de-coeur, tapping the crown of sonnets' template to explore modes of love – aspiration, longing, lust, etc. – that might be felt within a single relationship or, in this case, encounter. Use of the sonnet form implies a consistency of temperament across these modes, but each sonnet varies formally (Petrarchan, Shakespearean, Miltonic, etc.) conferring subtle differences in tone that make each mode – each emotional bedroom – unique.

Yvonne Blomer, "The Roll Call to the Ark"

"The Roll Call to the Ark" is a poem taken out of a series of poems called *The Birds of the Bible*. The poem is in two voices and was inspired by Genesis where first Noah is instructed to take two of each kind of male and female of every animal on to the ark and then later is instructed to take seven of clean and one of unclean animals.

Tim Bowling, "The Book Collector"

This poem did indeed take about twenty-seven minutes to write. Frost famously said that a poem ought to ride the force of its own melting, like an ice cube on a hot stove. A very busy domestic life basically collided *Titanic*-like with the ice cube of that idea, and "The Book Collector" was born. Of course, that explanation doesn't take into account how long I thought about the subject matter of the poem before I sat down to write, which simply proves that ideas about poetic composition, even by someone as brilliant as Frost, are usually beside the point.

Heather Cadsby, "One of us is in a Mohawk cemetery"

My great grandfather is the only white man buried in the Mohawk cemetery at Tyendinaga. He was a friend of the chief, Oronatekah.

Anne Compton, "Stars, Sunday Dawn"

The speaker of the poem is the younger sister of a boy who is an avid runner, especially on Sundays, the day of the week free from chores. He's turned every room of the house into a racecourse, but on Sundays he races – and she clocks him – in the biggest building on the farm, the granary. The poem pivots on the image of the girl holding the stopwatch. I've always thought running and writing a lot alike: both alter time. Obviously, in the course of this narrative poem, something happens to the boy.

Kevin Connolly, "Last One on the Moon"

As an offbeat, idiomatic, slightly surreal lyricist, I've always been more concerned that my poems be interesting or entertaining as opposed to profound or edifying. Imagine my horror, then, when I discovered at least a half-dozen references to the moon in my 2005 collection, *drift*. How could such a transparently overloaded image slip so easily under my defences? I adopted a self-imposed moratorium on the topic, until one evening, on my way home along the lake on my bicycle, I was hit in the face with an enormous, early-rising moon over Asbridge's Bay: completely extraterrestrial in every sense. The title, "Last One on the Moon," is probably wishful thinking, but I've held out since this poem – so far.

Méira Cook, "A Walker in the City"

In "A Walker in the City" I was interested in finding an appropriate poetic rhythm for the stride or saunter or amble; all the ways one has of moving through a claimed space, a city.

Dani Couture, "Union Station"

It arose out of the constant conflict experienced in living one foot in the city, one in the woods.

Sadiqa de Meijer, "There, there"

"There, there" was started during a month when I was moving and very oriented to what was going to happen; new city, new apartment, new work. I came across the planting instructions for poppies, and they caused me to consider what I was leaving – the poem grew from there.

Barry Dempster, "Blindness"

"Blindness" arose out of a trip to a stable north of Toronto where a very real one-eyed gelding named Sprout showered the author with curiosity and affection.

Jeramy Dodds, "The Gift"

"The Gift" comes from a long lineage of list poems. It has been informed by the landscape and rumours rampant throughout the Southern Ontario counties and lakefronts.

Jeffery Donaldson, "Museum"

I have for over a decade wanted to write a poem along the lines of the great ghostly encounter poems in the literature, where a living poet conjures the presence of a dead mentor and speaks through and with the projected voice about matters of pressing concern. Dante meets Virgil of course, T.S. Eliot encounters the compound ghost in "Little Gidding," James Merrill converses with the spirit of Auden in "The Changing Light at Sandover," and Seamus Heaney runs into the ghost of James Joyce at the end of "Station Island." These were stars to shoot for, not models I could hope to emulate. I always had Frye in mind as my spirit-mentor, but couldn't get the poem rolling until I realized that the conversation could be more about me, and my own habits of writing, than with Frye himself. Frye's good wisdom derives from different writings of his, but in particular a recommendation he makes on how children should be taught to write ... no rules at first, just lots of expressible energy.

Susan Elmslie, "Box"

I was thinking about this poem for years before writing it. I'd rehearse the scene in my head, trying to figure out what it meant to me personally as well as what shape it should take as a poem, so that it might be meaningful to others. Ultimately, I wanted to dramatize, in the form of a short (box-like) poem, the sort of narrative trajectory you see in a *Künstlerroman*, a story of becoming an artist. I wondered if there was an equivalent literary term for a poem concerned with the poet's *prise de conscience* and burgeoning recognition of the power of words – there ought to be.

Jason Guriel, "Spineless Sonnet"

I like poems that plunder what Eliot calls "the unexplored resources of the unpoetical." I don't know if a sock puppet is "unpoetical," but I'm not sure I've ever seen one in a sonnet. Anyway, there's a perverse thrill in writing about such a seemingly trivial thing in such a seemingly serious form.

Aurian Haller, "Song of the Taxidermist"

The poem, "Song of the Taxidermist," attempts to give voice to the body beyond the self's colonizing imperative. Rather than considering the flesh simply as a vehicle for transporting characters, each poetic episode treats its preserved specimen as a character in its own right.

Jason Heroux, "Lost Forest"

The first three lines entered, and the rest of the poem just kind of wonders what those lines might mean. I think the poem is about how our wilderness has disappeared, and so we've become our own wilderness. But we can't fill the void, and something inside us still continues to be lost, missing, and waiting to be found.

Iain Higgins, "A Digression on Hunting"

"A Digression on Hunting" might be thought of as a meditation on the complex relations between different states of being and doing, including waiting and wanting, making and unmaking, accepting and acting, creating and killing.

Bill Howell, "Late Light"

"Late Light" was written for my old friend, Carole Galloway, who was an actress and a painter. She died seven years ago at her home in Niagara-On-The-Lake.

Helen Humphreys, "Auden's House"

When I was a young writer, W.H. Auden was the poet I most admired. Years later, I had the chance to visit his house in Kirchstetten, Austria. In between my young self and the visit to the great poet's house, I had become disillusioned ¬ with poetry, and with myself. But getting a glimpse of the man Auden was, as I stood in his study at the top of his house, somehow gave me permission to argue with the self I had been when I first became a poet – the self I suddenly realized I no longer was.

Amanda Lamarche, "A Toast to Matthew, after Death"

"A Toast to Matthew, after Death" is from Amanda Lamarche's forthcoming second collection of poetry that is about, among other things, Lucy Maud Montgomery's fictional character, Matthew Cuthbert.

Tim Lilburn, "Orphic Hymn"

I wrote the poems in *Orphic Politics* between 2003 and 2007. This was a difficult time for me. I got quite ill, was hospitalized, and had a number of surgeries. I also developed an auto-immune condition that made walking difficult. I had never been sick like this before, never lived in the country of the ill, and my health problems went on for a couple of years. The poems respond to all of this. After a while, being sick felt like an orphic immurement. I began to think of other diseases in me that might be in need of healing, noological disorders – a loneliness for things, for example, the residue of colonialism. How to transform these? I subjected myself to the theurgic art of poetry.

Michael Lista, "The Scale of Intensity"

"The Scale of Intensity" was originally published in *Border Crossings* along with 13 other English-to-English translations from *Bloom*, a book of poems that follows Louis Slotin, the brilliant Winnipeg-born Manhattan Project physicist, who on May 21st 1946 lethally irradiated himself while preparing a plutonium core for criticality. It was written in the morning.

Keith Maillard, "July"

"July" is a sequence of twelve ghazals written in the form as it was introduced into Canadian poetry by John Thompson in his magnificent *Stilt Jack* (1978). Maillard wrote the first draft of "July" during the summer of 2002 when he was suffering from rapid atrial fibrillation – an irregularity of the heartbeat. After recovering, he continued to revise the sequence off and on for the next four years.

Don McKay, "Sleeping with the River"

A while back I spent the winter months living in the Haig-Brown House in Campbell River, BC, as writer in residence, with the Campbell flowing full tilt past the bedroom. As a sometime insomniac, I have the usual set of trick and technique for inducing sleep (the warm milk, the skullcap, the Valerian, the single malt, the heavy drugs). But I soon discovered that, what with the rains running through their scales and exercises and the river pouring out its blendered Berlitz, the affliction had thrown itself into reverse. I'd become a somniac. One of the many blessings of that remarkable place and time.

A.F. Moritz, "Odds and Ends"

"Odds and Ends" describes a painting by Emily Carr in the city art gallery of Victoria, and, more particularly, the experience in which my viewing of the painting was set. Leaving the gallery, I walked through the surrounding neighborhoods, thinking to come out soon on the ocean, but it turned out to be a long walk on a hot humid day: I'd misunderstood my map. And in a front yard I saw the rhododendron petal, and the pistils and stamens, naked of the petal, still above on their bush, as described. As for the "souvenir" dresses, they hang near my writing desk in an open closet, and it was in glimpsing them there, long after the Victoria experience, that the poem suddenly was written. John Barton, editor of the *Malahat Review*, helped me improve its ending, in emails responding to my disquiet about the then final lines, which are now gone. "Odds and Ends" was reprinted in my limited edition book *Sound of Hungry Animals* (Dublin, London, Toronto: Rufus Books, 2008), publisher Agnes Cserhati.

Jim Nason, "Chardin's Rabbit"

I wanted to write a poem about lilacs, and when the vision of the dead rabbit arrived I was shocked but decided to go wherever it took me. In the end, the poem is about the weirdness of betrayal; beauty in the grotesque; and the necessity of evoking mystery by paying attention to detail (I read and reread Bishop's "The Fish") in art.

Peter Norman, "Playground Incident"

"Playground Incident" is meant partly as an homage to the title and tone of Hwang JiWoo's "One Day I Will Sit Down in a Dim Pub," as translated from the Korean by Min Seong-bin.

Alison Pick, "The Dream World"

"The Dream World," the title poem of Alison Pick's most recent collection (McClelland & Stewart, 2008), explores the associative landscape of the subconscious, the rich and fertile world concealed behind the world we know and recognize.

E. Alex Pierce, "To float, to drown, to close up, to open – a throat"

The poem, "To float, to drown, to close up, to open – a throat" sprang from that opening line. The line came from a discarded poem that didn't make it into a manuscript. "[C]alling up out of a throat," an essential phrase from the earlier poem, stayed with me, and coalesced with a memory that disturbed me. I was at Banff for The Writing Studio (2007) and had the time to dwell on what tormented me: the sound of two old people, in the dark, at a kitchen table – from my childhood. The sound didn't torment me so much as the feeling that I was unable, or unwilling, to write about it. The memory of that sound was a prelude to the impulse to grasp what makes a voice a voice: Seamus Heaney's essay, "Feelings into Words," certainly lies at the bottom of this poem, and from it his insight into the "bedding of our language." Another source was my own annotation on a poem of Mary Oliver's ("White Owl Flies Into and Out of the Field") and her phrase, "…aortal light." I had carried the image of the anatomy of the aorta for a long, long time – and found a paper copy of that annotation when I was packing for Banff. Recognizing that my opening line was more than a line – a "throw" Don McKay calls it – and seeing in it a motif that would invite further exploration, gave me the possibility of a longer poem.

Craig Poile, "The Blanket"

The blanket that inspired the poem has, in fact, all the properties and history of its counterpart in the poem (such fidelity is unusual for me), and was bought many years ago by my spouse equivalent's late mother, Polly Smith. Only after writing the poem was I told, to my great happiness, that its final lines are borrowed from Elizabeth Barrett Browning's masterpiece, "Grief."

Matt Rader, "The Great Leap Forward"

I'm tempted to write that "The Great Leap Forward" has its provenance in the heat of a catastrophic love affair but that would be trite. More truthfully, like the sunflower and the bee, this poem organizes itself partly by way of Fibonacci numbers, that sequence of numbers first described in Sanskrit prosody that converges, as the numbers increase, on the omnipresent, yet elusive, "golden ratio."

Michael Eden Reynolds, "A-frame"

When I wrote the first draft of this poem it was the first new thing I'd written in nearly a year. It's kind of a true story. Sometime after writing it, I went back to the place with my son (then four) and he spotted a lynx. We watched it pad away into the trees.

Shane Rhodes, "If it was the sea we heard (Penelope's Song)"

"If it was the sea we heard (Penelope's Song)" is an accompanying piece to the introductory poem, "The Sea," in my last book *The Bindery*. Both poems attempt a bit of counterpunctal mimicry: sea sounds, repetition, rhyme, rhythm, questioning, and memory. They represent, for me, the beginning (and ending) of a 98 page voyage over unfamiliar (and yet familiar, for we are talking about Penelope from Homer's *Odyssey*, after all) seas. The seashore fascinates me – the start of so much life, death, mystery, and discovery, all of it in a continuous state of raveling and unraveling.

Joy Russell, "On King George's Crowning"

"On King George's Crowning" is part of a poetry manuscript whose eyes and ears fall on Vancouver, London and Belize, their bodies of water and connection to Empire.

Heather Sellers, "I Don't Remember Telling the Stepsons"

I am indebted to the poetry editor at PRISM for suggesting I cut the final stanza of this poem (it was another sixteen lines when I first sent it to PRISM). I love this last line and I would have never thought to end the poem there, with that accidentally brutal threat. I'm a fan of truncation and interruption. But we get so attached to our lines! Great editing. I wrote the poem in a state of boggled shame: my stepsons seemed to know all these horrifying things about my life. I must have told them these stories, but how could I have? I'm also interested in how what we remember, what others remember, and what we choose to tell have very little to do with each other. Craft-wise, there seem to be two kinds of poems – those that come out fairly whole and those that require work, work, work, great reconfigurings. This one, aside from the giant lop-off of its ending (it's like its hair was eight inches too long) came out fairly whole and that might be why I remain happy with it.

David Seymour, "Song for the Richardson's Ground Squirrel Whose Call is a Song for the Cry of the Short-Eared Owlet (They May One Day Meet for Dinner)"

"Song for the Richardson's Ground Squirrel..." is the result of notes written about my first encounter with the creatures in the prairies a few years ago. I found their habits and idiosyncrasies fascinating to watch, and sat for hours observing them. That same evening, I also came upon a nest of short-eared owlets, whose cries for food were eerily similar to the alert call of the squirrels.

J. Mark Smith, "Sweetness"

In the late 1990s, after I'd been living in California for nearly a decade, I got to know a couple who had a small, barely viable organic farm out in a very dry valley near the Nevada border. "Sweetness" was written later, in Toronto, when I was missing my former haunts. I meant the poem first of all to be a tribute to that desert place and to a mode of existence I admire.

Adam Sol, "Jeremiah Scrounges Rest"

This was a piece from my forthcoming book *Jeremiah, Ohio* that landed on the cutting room floor, for narrative reasons, so I'm very pleased that it's found a home elsewhere.

Carmine Starnino, "Squash Rackets"

"Squash Rackets" was based on a real game with poet Andrew Steinmetz. And yes, I got my ass handed to me.

Anna Swanson, "Morning After"

That first summer in St. John's was full of surprises: I slept with a man for the first time in a decade, started to drink beer again, began my long fall off the wagon of vegetarianism, picked my first wild blueberries, managed somehow to break the first condom I'd used in ten years. Anything seemed possible.

Todd Swift, "Gentlemen of Nerve"

"Gentlemen of Nerve" gets its title from a Charlie Chaplin silent film from 1914 – there is also a reference to the Laurel and Hardy comedy *A Chump at Oxford* in the poem. I wrote the poem around the time of my father's death – I'd turned 40 – and was thinking about how he used to take me to see old comedies, like *Modern Times*, when I was a kid. I knew that "poet turns 40, mourns dad" poems were a potential pitfall – but slapstick is full of such things. I'd been a screenwriter, and, living in the leafy London area of Maida Vale (near Notting Hill), found myself strolling to cafes, musing on life, and feeling a bit like a Chaplin character myself – semi-bum, semi-boulevardier. So, this flaneur poem came together, as my poems often do, suddenly, and just flowed. I am not sure how all the "science" got into it, but I felt it should be a real 20th century poem, stylish, confessional, and erudite. It seems to have hit a nerve (it's one readers react to) and I am pleased with that. The sad truths working through the poem, becoming realized in the process, are also the lively, lovely strands that make life worth living.

E. Leif Vaage, "Shrove Tuesday"

The poem describes an early spring day moving between Guysborough and Peas Brook and, then, at Peas Brook on the Chedaducto Day. It traces the fine line between praise and angst, the open horizon of new life and the unresolved pain of the lingering past, the delights of purgatory.

LONG LIST OF 50 POEMS

1. Armstrong, Tammy. "Canoe Lessons." *Contemporary Verse 2.* Summer 2007. Vol. 30, No. 1. 117.

2. Avasilichioaei, Oana. "Origins of The Book of Questions." *The Capilano Review.* 3:3. 95–104.

3. Bachinsky, Elizabeth. "On Spiders: Barbarian Press, Steelhead, British Columbia." *Matrix* 78. 43.

4. Barrett, Adrienne. "You walk into the dance." *Prairie Fire.* Vol 28, No 1. 64.

5. Barwin, Gary. "Fish of Rage." *This Magazine.* March/April 2007. 37.

6. Bemrose, John. "The Eyes Have It." *The Walrus.* October 2007.

7. Browne, Heather. "Patternings No. 6." *Descant* 137. 124.

8. Carr, Angela. "of running, of the core." *Capilano Review.* 3:3. 35.

9. Clewes, Rosemary. "Lookout." *Fiddlehead* 231. 94.

10. Conn, Jan. "Minotaur." *Literary Review of Canada.* Vol 15, No 1. Jan/Feb 2007. 16.

11. Cookshaw, Marlene. "Heaven (Oregon, 1993)." *Arc* 59. 22–3.

12. Crymble, Phillip, "Port Authority." *Malahat Review* 161. 85.

13. Di Nardo, Antony. "On the Moroccan coast (granted in a purple haze)." *Lichen.* Spring/Summer 2007. 21.

14. Funk, Carla. "Summer Afternoon, Lying in the Grass." *Fiddlehead* 233. 43.

15. Garnett, Heidi. "Broken Off." *Antigonish Review* 151. 21–22.

16. Neilsen Glenn, Lorri. "Sunday Morning." *Arc* 59. 21.

17. Grubisic, Katia. "Basin No. 3." *Contemporary Verse 2.* Autumn 2007. 64.

18. Harrison, Douglas. "Caught in a Downpour." *Event.* 36: 2. 26.

19. Heiti, Warren. "Rain Sutra." *Prism International.* 46: 1. 43.

20. Hofmann, Karen. "Long Beach." *Fiddlehead* 233. 88.

21. Holmes, Matthew, "Glazier." *New Quarterly* 104. Fall 2007. 134.

22. Lebowitz, Rachel. "The Locomotive (1) and (2)." *Fiddlehead* 230. 47.

23. Leckie, Ross. "The Old Shoes, the New Shoes." *Qwerty* 21. Spring 2007. 105.

24. Leigh, Simon. "Fabulous Fifties Fashions." *Descant* 138. Fall 2007. 41–2.

25. Madden, Rob. "Auto Assembly." *Grain*. Vol 35, No 1. Summer 2007. 46.

26. McCartney, Sharon. "Lady Ashley." *Lichen*. Spring/Summer 2007. 40.

27. Minkus, Kim. "9 Freight." *WestCoast Line*. 52. 16–24.

28. Murakami, Sachiko. "Monster (Dead Duck)." *Event*. 36:2. 35.

29. Noyes, Steve. "The Blossoms of Chang'an." *Contemporary Verse 2*. Vol 29, No 3. 45–6.

30. Page, P.K. "Hughes." *Malahat Review* 161. 30.

31. Pass, John. "Finally." *Malahat Review* 160. Fall 2007. 123.

32. Quartermain, Meredith. "Frontier." *WestCoast Line 54*. 38.

33. Reibetanz, John. "Diminuendo on the Theme of Whether Shakespeare's Monument Bears of True Likeness." *Literary Review of Canada*. Vol 15, No 10. December 2007. 17.

34. Rhenisch, Harold. "The Bone Yard." *Malahat Review* 159. 44–56.

35. Robinson, Matt. "historic properties & the like." *Antigonish Review* 150. 9.

36. Rotstein, Jason Ranon Uri. "Before and After." *Literary Review of Canada*. Vol 15. No 6. 17.

37. Ruzesky, Jay. "While You Were Out." *Arc* 59. 42–43.

38. Schneiders, Jay. "The Grass Is." *Descant* 137. 110.

39. Smith, Hillary. "Jasper." *Contemporary Verse 2*. Vol 29, No 3. 90.

40. Solie, Karen. "The Weather Channel." *Qwerty* 21. Spring 2007. 70.

41. Sutherland, Fraser. "On a Drawing by Paul Young." *Literary Review of Canada*. Vol 15, No 2. March 2007. 14.

42. Strimas, Meaghan. "Shotgun Wedding." *Exile*. Vol 30, No 4.

43. Thesen, Sharon. "The Consumptives of Tranquille Sanatorium, 1953." *Capilano Review*. Vol 3, No 1-2. 227–30.

44. Thran, Nick. "Amanda is the Sunshine That Keeps The Plants Alive." *Grain*. Vol 34, No 3. Winter 2007.

45. Tierney, Matthew. "Love Triangle." *Arc* 59. 44–5.

46. Timmers, Kate. "Wright 1." *Antigonish Review* 151. 102.

47. Vermeersch, Paul. "Altarpiece with False Teeth and Parkinson's Disease." *Event.* 35:3. 49–50.

48. Warner, Patrick. "Coronation Street." *Fiddlehead* 230. 57–8.

49. Wolff, Elana. "Helleborus." *Taddle Creek.* Christmas Number 2007. 52.

50. Yorke, Stephanie. "Rita (and Jack's), Tomato Season." *Fiddlehead* 233. 47.

SHORT LIST POETS' BIOGRAPHIES

MALEEA ACKER is a writer, publisher (of La Mano Izquierda/Left Hand Press), typographer, translator and English instructor. Her first full length collection of poetry, *The Reflecting Pool*, will appear with Pedlar Press in the Spring of 2009.

JAMES ARTHUR's poems have appeared or are forthcoming in *The New Yorker*, *The New Republic*, *The Nation*, *Brick*, and *The Southern Review*. He has held fellowships at Yaddo and the MacDowell Colony, and from 2006 to 2007, he was the Amy Lowell Traveling Poetry Scholar. He lives in Toronto but is currently a Stegner Fellow in Poetry at Stanford University. He is married to writer Shannon Robinson.

LEANNE AVERBACH is a Canadian text and performance poet and video artist. She has been published and has performed with musicians across Canada, in the US, and in Italy. Her first book *Fever* (Mansfield Press, Toronto) was short-listed for the national Gerald Lampert Memorial first poetry book prize in 2006. Her companion CD *Fever* is a fusion of her spoken words and the blues/jazz accompaniment of the Vancouver group, Indigo. *The Georgia Straight* writes of the CD, "The poems swing from worldly to wild." Averbach's first video-poem *Carwash* can be viewed at www.leanneaverbach.com or http://ca.youtube.com/leanneaverbach. Her second short film, *Teacups & Mink*, recently screened at the New York International Independent Film & Video Festival 2008, and was selected as Best Short International Film, Poetic Genre, as well as Best Short Film at the Palm Desert Film Festival. For more information go to www.leanneaverbach.com.

MARGARET AVISON's work has, over the course of a career spanning four decades, won numerous awards, including two Governor General's Awards and, for *Concrete and Wild Carrot*, the Griffin Poetry Prize. Her books of poetry include *Always Now: The Collected Poems* and, most recently, *Momentary Dark*. Margaret Avison died in July 2007, in Toronto. Her final collection, *Listening: the Last Poems of Margaret Avison*, will be published posthumously by McClelland & Stewart in Spring, 2009.

KEN BABSTOCK is the author of *Mean* (1999), winner of The Atlantic Poetry Prize and Milton Acorn Award, *Days into Flatspin* (2001), winner of a K.M. Hunter Award and shortlisted for the Winterset Prize, and, most recently *Airstream Land Yacht* (2006), which was a finalist for the Governor General's Award, The Winterset Prize, The Griffin Prize, and won The Trillium Award for Poetry. All three were Globe and Mail Books of The Year. Babstock's poems have been translated into Dutch, German, French, and Serbo-Croatian. He lives in Toronto where he works as a writer, editor, and teacher.

JOHN WALL BARGER was born on Staten Island, New York, in 1969, and moved to Nova Scotia when he was seven. Educated at Simon Fraser University and Carleton, he has lived in Rome, Prague, Dublin, and now Halifax, where he teaches English literature part time at Saint Mary's University. In 2008, his poems appeared in *Descant*, *Grain*, *CV2*, *The Antigonish Review*, and *The Malahat Review*.

BRIAN BARTLETT of Halifax has published many books and chapbooks of poems, including *The Watchmaker's Table* (Goose Lane, 2008), *The Afterlife of Trees* (McGill-Queens, 2002), and *Wanting the Day: Selected Poems* (2003), which was published by Goose Lane in Canada and by Peterloo Poets in Britain, and won the Atlantic Poetry Prize. Bartlett has also edited a book of prose, *Don McKay: Essays on His Works*, and two volumes of selected poems, *Earthly Pages: The Poetry of Don Domanski* and (forthcoming) *The Essential James Reaney*.

JOHN BARTON has published eight books of poetry and five chapbooks, including *Sweet Ellipsis* (1998), and *Hypothesis* (2001). A bilingual edition of his third book, *West of Darkness: Emily Carr, a self-portrait*, was published in 2006; his ninth collection, *Hymn*, is forthcoming from Brick in 2009. Co-editor of *Seminal: The Anthology of Canada's Gay-Male Poets* (2007), he has won three Archibald Lampman Awards, a Patricia Hackett Prize, an Ottawa Book Award, a 2003 CBC Literary Award, and a 2006 National Magazine Award. The former editor of Ottawa's *Arc*, he lives in Victoria, where he edits *The Malahat Review*. In 2008–2009, he is writer in residence at Saskatoon Public Library.

YVONNE BLOMER's poetry has appeared in literary journals in Canada and abroad. Her first collection, *a broken mirror, fallen leaf*, was short listed for the Gerald Lampert Memorial Award. Her work has been included in *Rocksalt: An Anthology of Contemporary BC Poetry* and *In Fine Form: The Canadian Book of Form Poetry*. Yvonne lives in Victoria, BC, where she writes poetry and reviews and teaches courses in writing.

TIM BOWLING has published seven poetry collections, including *Low Water Slack*; *Dying Scarlet* (winner of the 1998 Stephan G. Stephansson Award for poetry); *Darkness and Silence* (winner of the Canadian Authors Association Award for Poetry); *The Witness Ghost*; and *The Memory Orchard* (both nominated for the Governor General's Literary Award). He is also the author of three novels, *Downriver Drift* (Harbour), *The Paperboy's Winter* (Penguin) and *The Bone Sharps* (Gaspereau Press). His first book of nonfiction, *The Lost Coast: Salmon, Memory and the Death of Wild Culture* (Nightwood Editions), was shortlisted for three literary awards: The Writers' Trust Nereus Non-Fiction Award, the BC Book Prizes' Roderick Haig-Brown Regional Prize and the Alberta Literary Awards' Wilfred Eggleston Award for Non-Fiction. *The Lost Coast* was also chosen as a 2008 Kiriyama Prize "Notable Book." Bowling is the recipient of the Petra Kenney International Poetry Prize, the National Poetry Award, and the Orillia International Poetry Prize. Bowling was the recipient of a Guggenheim Fellowship in 2008. A native of the West Coast, he now lives in Edmonton Alberta.

HEATHER CADSBY lives in Toronto. She is the author of three books of poetry. *A Tantrum of Synonyms* (Wolsak and Wynn) was a finalist for the Pat Lowther Award. Her fourth book, titled *Could be*, will be published in 2009 by Brick Books.

ANNE COMPTON is the author of *Processional* (2005), winner of the Governor General's Award for Poetry and the Atlantic Poetry Prize, and shortlisted for the Pat Lowther Award; and *Opening the Island* (2002), winner of the Atlantic Poetry Prize and shortlisted for the John and Margaret Savage Award. She is the author as well of the scholarly works – *A.J.M. Smith: Canadian Metaphysical* (1994) and *Meetings with Maritime Poets: Interviews* (2006). Compton is the editor of *The Edge of Home: Milton Acorn from the Island* (2002) and co-editor of *Coastlines: The Poetry of Atlantic Canada* (2002). In 2008, she won The Alden Nowlan Award for Excellence in the Literary Arts and a National Magazine Award (silver).

KEVIN CONNOLLY is a Toronto poet, editor and arts journalist. He has published four full-length collections, including *drift* (Anansi), which won the 2005 Trillium Poetry Award, and most recently, *Revolver* (Anansi, 2008). He is the poetry editor for Coach House books.

MÉIRA COOK has had numerous books published, including *Slovenly Love*, published by Brick Books in 2003, and a book of critical essays, *Writing Lovers: Reading Canadian Love Poetry By Women* published by McGill-Queen's University Press in 2005. One of the poems in *A Walker in the City* is currently appearing on a bus card on the #36 city bus in Winnipeg.

DANI COUTURE is the author of *Good Meat* (Pedlar Press, 2006). She is co-editor of *Northern Poetry Review* and the creator of Animal Effigy. Her second book of poetry, *The Handbook*, is forthcoming from Pedlar Press.

SADIQA DE MEIJER's poems have appeared in *The Malahat Review*, *The Antigonish Review* and *Geist*, and one of them won first prize in *This Magazine*'s Great Canadian Literary Hunt. Her writing has also won Other Voices' Short Fiction Contest, and the CBC's Ontario Today Playwriting Competition.

BARRY DEMPSTER is the author of 9 collections of poetry, two of which have been nominated for the Governor General's Award. His most recent publication, *The Burning Alphabet*, also won the Canadian Authors Association Chalmers Award for Poetry. He has two new books forthcoming: *Love Outlandish* with Brick Books in 2009 and *Ivan's Birches* with Pedlar Press in 2010. Dempster is senior editor at Brick Books.

JERAMY DODDS lives in Orono, Ontario. His first collection of poems, *Crabwise to the Hounds*, will be published in the fall of 2008 by Coach House Books.

JEFFERY DONALDSON teaches poetry in the English department at McMaster University. He has published three volumes of poems: *Once Out of Nature* (McClelland & Stewart, 1991); *Waterglass* (McGill Queen's, 1999), and *Palilalia* (McGill-Queen's, 2008). He has edited a volume of essays entitled *Frye and the Word: Religious Contexts in the writings of Northrop Frye*, (U of T Press, 2004). His home overlooks Lake Ontario from the Niagara

Escarpment near Grimsby, where he lives with his wife Annette Abma and children Miller and Cory.

SUSAN ELMSLIE's first collection of poetry, *I, Nadja, and Other Poems* (Brick, 2006) won the A.M. Klein Poetry Prize and was shortlisted for the McAuslan First Book Prize, the Pat Lowther Award, and a ReLit Award. Her poems have also appeared in several journals, anthologies, and in a prize-winning chapbook, *When Your Body Takes to Trembling* (Cranberry Tree, 1996). She has been a poetry Fellow at Hawthornden Castle in Scotland. She lives in Montreal with her husband and two young children and teaches English at Dawson College. www.susanelmslie.org

JASON GURIEL is the recipient of the Frederick Bock Prize from *Poetry* magazine. His second collection of poems will be published by Véhicule Press in 2009. He lives in Toronto.

Poet and singer-songwriter, AURIAN HALLER, lives in Quebec City with his wife and two children. He is a National Magazine Award winner for 2008, and co-winner of the 2007 Malahat Review Long Poem Prize. His poems have been published in Canada, the US, Ireland, and Australia. Aurian's first book, *A Dream of Sulphur*, was published in 2000. He is currently completing his next book, *Song of the Taxidermist*.

JASON HEROUX lives in Kingston Ontario. He is the author of two poetry collections published by Mansfield Press, *Memoirs of an Alias* (2004) and *Emergency Hallelujah* (2008).

IAIN HIGGINS is the author of *Then Again* (Oolichan, 2005) and the translator of *The Invention of Poetry, the selected poems of Adam Czerniawski* (Salt, 2005). His poems have appeared in *The New Canon* (2005) and in magazines such as *Canadian Literature, Descant, Fiddlehead*, and *Malahat Review*. New work will appear in *Rocksalt: An Anthology of Contemporary BC Poetry* (forthcoming). He lives in Victoria.

BILL HOWELL was a network CBC Radio Drama producer-director for almost three decades until the cuts caught up to him. He has three full collections and his work appears regularly in Canadian literary journals. *Ghost Test Flights* (Rubicon Press) is one of the winners of this year's WCDR Chapbook Challenge. Upcoming work includes a feature in *New Quarterly*, a seven-part serial piece in *Descant*, a pair of Mother Corp escapades in *Rampike*, and his debut in *The New York Quarterly*.

HELEN HUMPHREYS is the author of four books of poetry (*Gods and Other Mortals; Nuns Looking Anxious, Listening to Radios; The Perils of Geography; Anthem*) – five novels (*Leaving Earth; Afterimage; The Lost Garden; Wild Dogs; Coventry*) – and one work of nonfiction (*The Frozen Thames*). She lives and writes in Kingston, Ontario.

AMANDA LAMARCHE, originally from Smooth Rock Falls, ON, moved to Gibsons, BC, when she was 11 years old. She has received a BA in English from the University of Victoria and an MFA in Creative Writing from the University of British Columbia. Her work has been published in numerous magazines and anthologized in *Breathing Fire 2: Canada's New Poets*. Her first poetry collection, *The Clichéist*, was published by Nightwood Editions in 2005. Most recently, she has moved to Summerside, Prince Edward Island, where she works as a medical transcriptionist.

TIM LILBURN was born in Regina, Saskatchewan. He now lives in British Columbia, where he teaches at the University of Victoria. His most recent books are *Orphic Politics* (McClelland & Stewart) and a book of essays, *Going Home* (Anansi).

MICHAEL LISTA has published most recently in *The Malahat Review*, *Canadian Literature*, and the art magazine *Border Crossings*. He was a finalist for the *Malahat Review* Long Poem Prize, the *Descant*/Winston Collins Prize, and has twice been nominated for a Pushcart Prize. His debut, *Bloom*, is forthcoming from The House of Anansi. He lives in Montreal's Mile End.

KEITH MAILLARD was born and raised in Wheeling, West Virginia, and emigrated to Canada in 1970. He is the author of thirteen novels and one book of poetry, *Dementia Americana*, which won the Gerald Lampert award for the best first book of poetry published in Canada in 1995. Maillard is a Professor at the University of British Columbia where he is currently the Chair of the Creative Writing Program. He lives in Vancouver with his wife and two daughters.

DON MCKAY's most recent books are *Camber* and *Strike/Slip* (McClelland & Stewart) and *Deactivated West 100* (Gaspereau Press). He currently resides in Newfoundland.

A. F. MORITZ's book of poems, *The Sentinel*, was published by House of Anansi Press in April 2008. His poetry has received awards including the Guggenheim Fellowship, the Ingram Merrill Fellowship, the Award in Literature of the American Academy and Institute of Arts and Letters, and the Beth Hokin Prize of *Poetry* magazine. *Night Street Repairs* (House of Anansi Press, 2004) won the 2005 ReLit Award for poetry, and *Rest on the Flight into Egypt* (Brick Books, 1999) was a finalist for the Governor General's Award in literature. His poems have appeared in four editions of the annual *Best American Poetry* series and in Harold Bloom's 1998 *Best of the Best American Poetry*.

JIM NASON's stories and poems have been published in numerous journals and anthologies in Canada and the United States. He is the author of two collections of poetry: *If Lips Were as Red* (Palmerston Press) and *The Fist of Remembering* (Wolsak and Wynn). "Chardin's Rabbit" is from his new collection, *Laneway Home* (forthcoming). In 2007, his novel, *The Housekeeping Journals*, was published by Turnstone Press. He holds an MA in English Literature from McGill University as well as degrees from Ryerson and York Universities. Currently he lives and works in Toronto.

PETER NORMAN's poetry has appeared in numerous literary journals – including *The Malahat Review*, *The Fiddlehead* and *Prairie Fire* – and the anthology *Jailbreaks: 99 Canadian Sonnets*. Once, as a young child, he was disproportionately disturbed by the sight of a snapped swing.

ALISON PICK is the author of the novel, *The Sweet Edge*, a Globe and Mail Top 100 Book of 2005. Her poetry collection, *Question & Answer*, was a finalist for the Gerald Lampert Award for Best First Book and for a Newfoundland and Labrador Book Award. Alison has also won the 2002 Bronwen Wallace Award, the 2003 National Magazine Award, and the 2005 CBC Literary Award.

E. ALEX PIERCE is a native of Nova Scotia where she divides her time between Sydney, Cape Breton and East Sable River on the South Shore. Her work has been published in a number of Canadian literary journals (*Arc*, *CV2*, *Fiddlehead*, *The New Quarterly*) and anthologized in *Words Out There: Women Poets in Atlantic Canada* (Roseway) and in *The Hoodoo You Do So Well: Poetry From The Banff Writing Studio 2007* (little fishcartpress). Her poem, "Sestina on Six Words from Frances Itani's *Deafening*," was broadcast for CBC Sydney's Radio One Program, *Canada Reads: Ask the Poets* (2006). Her long poem, "Snow White & Rose Red" was shortlisted for the CBC Literary Awards in 2004; "Two Houses," a segment from "To float, to drown, to close up, to open – a throat," was shortlisted in 2007. The opening section of "To float, to drown..." was awarded First Honourable Mention in *Arc*'s Poem of the Year Competition 2007 and is published in *Arc* #59. She has twice been a participant in The Banff Centre's Writing Studio, most recently in spring, 2007. She holds an MFA in Creative Writing from Warren Wilson College, North Carolina, and teaches creative writing (playwriting and poetry) at Cape Breton University where she is Assistant Professor. Recently she has been named editor for the CBU Press series, The Essential Cape Breton Library.

CRAIG POILE lives in Ottawa, where he works as a technical writer and is co-owner of Collected Works Bookstore. His poems have recently appeared in *Canadian Notes & Queries* (CNQ) and *Seminal: The Anthology of Canada's Gay Male Poets*.

MATT RADER is the author of two books of poems: *Miraculous Hours* (2005) and *Living Things* (2008). His poems, stories, and nonfiction have appeared in journals and anthologies across North America, Australia, and Europe and have been nominated for numerous awards including the Gerald Lampert Award, the Journey Prize, and two Pushcart Prizes.

Born in 1973 in Ottawa, MICHAEL EDEN REYNOLDS grew up in Caledon, Ontario. Since 1995 he's lived in Whitehorse with his wife Jenny. They have two kids. Michael's poems have been published in magazines across Canada. In 2005 he received the Ralph Gustafson Prize. His long poem *Fugue* (in various incarnations) was a finalist in the 2005

CBC Literary Awards, the 2006 Bronwen Wallace Memorial Award, and *The Malahat Review*'s 2007 Long Poem Contest. Michael's chapbook, *Migrations*, was published by Linnaea Press (Whitehorse) in 2001. His first book, *Slant Room*, will be published by The Porcupine's Quill in Spring 2009.

SHANE RHODES's most recent book of poetry, *The Bindery*, was published by NeWest Press in 2007. Winner of an Alberta Book Award and the Archibald Lampman Award, Shane's poetry is also featured in the anthologies *New Canadian Poetry*, *Breathing Fire 2*, *Decalogue*, and *Seminal: Canada's Gay Male Poets*.

Born in Belize, JOY RUSSELL is a poet, writer and playwright. Her writing has appeared in *The Capilano Review*, *Crab Orchard*, *Callaloo*, *The Caribbean Writer*, *Beyond the Pale: Dramatic Writing from First Nation Writers and Writers of Colour*, *Velocity: The Best of Apples and Snakes*, *IC3: The Penguin Book of New Black Writing in Britain* and *Blueprint: Black British Columbian Literature and Orature*. She lived in London, England for many years working as an assistant producer and researcher on documentaries and currently lives in North Vancouver.

HEATHER SELLERS is the author of three volumes of poetry, most recently *The Boys I Borrow*. Her collection of short stories is *Georgia Under Water*, and she's written several popular books on the writing process as well as a textbook for creative writing classrooms. Her website is heathersellers.com.

DAVID SEYMOUR's first book of poetry, *Inter Alia* published by Brick Books, was nominated for the 2005 Gerald Lampert Award. His poetry, reviews, and essays have also appeared in *Fiddlehead*, *The Malahat Review*, *Arc*, *Prism International*, *Precipice*, and *Ellipse*, among others. David lives in Toronto and is currently at work on his second and third books.

J. MARK SMITH lives in Edmonton, and teaches at Grant MacEwan College. His first book of poems, *Notes for a Rescue Narrative*, was published by Oolichan in 2007.

ADAM SOL is the author of two collections of poetry: *Jonah's Promise* and *Crowd of Sounds*, which won Ontario's Trillium Award for Poetry in 2004. His third book, *Jeremiah, Ohio*, will be published this fall by House of Anansi Press. He is also the author of numerous essays and reviews for publications as various as the *Globe and Mail*, *The Forward*, *Bookninja. com* and *Shofar*. He lives in Toronto and teaches in the Laurentian University at Georgian College program.

CARMINE STARNINO is the author of three books of poems, including *With English Subtitles* (Gaspereau Press, 2004) and a collection of essays about Canadian poetry, *A Lover's Quarrel* (Porcupine's Quill, 2004). A new poetry collection, *This Way Out*, is forthcoming from Gaspereau Press in spring 2009.

ANNA SWANSON lives in Vancouver, BC, where she works as a children's librarian. She studied creative writing at the University of Victoria and sometimes pays the phone bill with poetry. In 2007 her poetry was published in *Room*, *The Antigonish Review*, *Prairie Fire*, and *The Torah: A Women's Commentary*.

TODD SWIFT was born in Montreal, on Good Friday, 1966, and grew up in St-Lambert, Quebec. His poems have appeared in the anthologies *The New Canon* and *Open Field*, and in numerous publications, such as *The Guardian*, *Poetry London*, and *Poetry Review*. He is the editor of several international poetry anthologies, including *Poetry Nation*, *Short Fuse*, and *100 Poets Against The War*; and the poetry editor of online magazine *Nthposition*. In 2005, he edited a special section on The Young Canadian Poets for *New American Writing*. He is a contributing editor for *Matrix* and *Mimesis*. He has had four full collections of poems out from DC Books in Montreal (*Budavox*, 1999; *Cafe Alibi*, 2002; *Rue du Regard*, 2004; and *Winter Tennis*, 2007). His *New and Selected* is out from Salmon Publishing, Ireland, in November 2008. As Oxfam Great Britain's first Poet-in-Residence, 2004–2008, he ran the Oxfam Poetry Series, and edited the bestselling CDs, *Life Lines* and *Life Lines 2 – Poets for Oxfam*. In 1997, Swift moved to Budapest, then to Paris in 2001. A graduate of the MA in Creative Writing at UEA, he is a core tutor with The Poetry School, and creative writing lecturer at Kingston University. He now lives and works in London, England, with his Irish wife, Sara.

J.R. TORISEVA has been awarded the Mary Merritt Henry Prize in Poetry and a working scholarship from the Bread Load Writers' Conference and has been published in *PRISM International*, *14 Hills*, *CV2* and *Fulcrum*. Toriseva has studied with Anne Carson, Sylvia Legris, Roo Borson and Betsy Struthers.

LEIF E. VAAGE teaches at Victoria University (Emmanuel College) in Toronto, Ontario. He lives in Halifax, Nova Scotia, and especially Guysborough and Peas Brook on the Chedabucto Bay. Born and raised in British Columbia, he studied in the United States and then became someone else in Lima, Perú, where he continues to collaborate with different projects. He may be reached at: leif.vaage@utoronto.ca.

MAGAZINES WHERE THE POEMS
WERE FIRST PUBLISHED

1. Acker, Maleea. "The Reflecting Pool." *Prism International.* 45:3. 53.

2. James Arthur, "Americans." *Brick.* Summer 2007.

3. Averbach, Leanne. "To the Lighthouse." *Contemporary Verse 2.* Autumn 2007. 61.

4. Avison, Margaret. "Hag-Ridden." *Prism International.* 46:1. 68.

5. Babstock, Ken. "Hunter Deary and Hospital Wing." *Matrix* 77. 12.

6. Barger, John Wall. "Weather." *Contemporary Verse 2.* Vol 30, No 1.

7. Bartlett, Brian. "Dear Georgie." *Malahat Review* 158. 15.

8. Barton, John. "One Bedroom Apartment." *Event* 36:2. 7–13.

9. Blomer, Yvonne. "The Roll Call to the Ark." *Descant* 136. Spring 2007. 212–4.

10. Bowling, Tim "The Book Collector." *Fiddlehead* 231. 7–9.

11. Cadsby, Heather. "One of us is in a Mohawk Cemetery." *Prism International.* 45:4. 69.

12. Compton, Anne. "Stars, Sunday Dawn." *Malahat Review* 161. 17.

13. Connolly, Kevin. "Last One on the Moon." *Maisonneuve* 25. 13.

14. Cook, Méira. "A Walker in the City." *En Route.* May 2007. 107–110.

15. Couture, Dani. "Union Station." *THIS Magazine.* November/December 2007. 42.

16. De Meijer, Sadiqa. "There, there." *Malahat Review* 161. 24.

17. Dempster, Barry. "Blindness." *Contemporary Verse 2.* Vol 30, No 1. 39–40.

18. Dodds, Jeramy. "The Gift." *Arc* 59. 48–49.

19. Donaldson, Jeffery. "Museum." *Antigonish Review* 151. 69–74.

20. Elmslie, Susan. "Box." *Arc* 59. 12.

21. Guriel, Jason. "Spineless Sonnet." *Maisonneuve* 25. 41.

22. Haller, Aurian. "Song of the Taxidermist." *Malahat Review* 159. 5–20.

23. Heroux, Jason. "Lost Forest." *Exile.* Vol 30, No 4.

24. Higgins, Iain. "A Digression on Hunting." *Fiddleheaad* 231. 49.

25. Howell, Bill. "Late Light." *Canadian Literature* 193. 53.

26. Humphreys, Helen. "Auden's House." *Malahat Review* 159. 64–5.

27. Lamarche, Amanda. "A Toast to Matthew, after Death." *Prairie Fire*. Vol 28, No 3. 24.

28. Lilburn, Tim. "Orphic Hymn." *Arc* 59. 68.

29. Lista, Michael. "The Scale of Intensity." *Border Crossings* 104. 78.

30. Maillard, Keith. "July." *Event*. 35:3. 60–71.

31. McKay, Don. "Sleeping with the River." *Brick*. Winter 2007. 73.

32. Moritz, A.F. "Odds and Ends." *Malahat Review* 161. 36.

33. Nason, Jim. "Chardin's Rabbit." *Descant* 136. Spring 2007. 211.

34. Norman, Peter. "Playground Incident." *Descant* 136. 110–111.

35. Pick, Alison. "The Dream World." *Grain*. Vol 34, No 4. Spring 2007. 15.

36. Pierce, E. Alex, "To float, to drown, to close up, to open – a throat." *Arc* 59. 16–19.

37. Poile, Craig. "The Blanket." *Literary Review of Canada*. Vol 15, No 2. March 2007. 15.

38. Rader, Matt. "The Great Leap Forward." *Prism International*. 46:1. 35–6.

39. Reynolds, Michael Eden. "A-frame." *Prism International*. 45:4. 71.

40. Rhodes, Shane. "If it was the sea we heard." *Canadian Literature* 192. Spring 2007. 95–6.

41. Russell, Joy. "On King George's Crowning." *Capilano Review*. 3:3 52–3.

42. Sellers, Heather. "I Don't Remember Telling the Stepsons." *Prism International*. 45:2. 33–4.

43. Seymour, David. "Song for the Richardson's Ground Squirrel Whose Call is a Song for the Cry of the Short-Eared Owlet (They May One Day Meet for Dinner)." *Malahat Review* 158. 25.

44. Smith, J. Mark. "Sweetness." *Fiddlehead* 231. 55–7.

45. Sol, Adam. "Jeremiah Scrounges Rest." *Fiddlehead* 231. 95.

46. Starnino, Carmine. "Squash Rackets." *Fiddlehead* 231. 31–2.

47. Swanson, Anna. "Morning after." *Room*. 30.2.

48. Swift, Todd. "Gentlemen of Nerve." *Vallum.* 4:2 / 5:1. 16–7.

49. Toriseva, J.R. "Encyclopedia of Grass." *Fiddlehead* 231. 82–3.

50. Vaage, Leif E. "Shrove Tuesday." *Fiddlehead* 233. 92.

MAGAZINES CONSIDERED FOR 2008 EDITION

The Antigonish Review

P.O. Box 5000
Antigonish, NS B2G 2W5
Tel: (902) 867-3962
Fax: (902) 867-5563
E-mail: tar@stfx.ca
http://www.antigonishreview.com/

Arc: Canada's National Poetry Magazine

P.O. Box 81060
Ottawa, ON K1P 1B1
http://www.arcpoetry.ca/

Brick: A Literary Journal

Box 609, Stn. P
Toronto, ON M5S 2Y4
http://www.brickmag.com/

Books in Canada
[did not publish any poetry in 2007]

The Canadian Review of Books Ltd.
6021 Yonge St., Ste. 1014
Toronto, ON M2M 3W2
Tel: (416) 222-7139
Fax: (416) 222-9384
E-mail: olga.stein@rogers.com
http://www.booksincanada.com/

Border Crossings

500–70 Arthur St.
Winnipeg, MB R3B 1G7
http://www.bordercrossingsmag.com/

Contemporary Verse 2: The Canadian Journal of Poetry and Critical Writing

207–100 Arthur St.
Winnipeg, MB R3B 1H3
Tel: (204) 949-1365
Fax: (204) 942-5754
E-mail: cv2@mts.net
http://www.contemporaryverse2.ca/

Canadian Literature

University of British Columbia
1866 Main Mall – E158
Vancouver, BC V6Y 1Z1
Tel: (604) 822-2780
Fax: (604) 822-5504
E-mail: can.lit@ubc.ca
http://www.canlit.ca/

The Capilano Review

2055 Purcell Way
North Vancouver, BC V7J 3H5
Tel: (604) 984-1712
E-mail: contact@thecapilanoreview.ca
http://www.thecapilanoreview.ca/

Dandelion Magazine

http://www.dandelionmagazine.ca/

Descant

PO Box 314, Stn. P
Toronto, ON M5S 2S8
E-mail: info@descant.ca
http://www.descant.ca/

En Route Magazine

Spafax Canada
4200 boul. St-Laurent, Ste. 707
Montreal, QC H2W 2R2
Tel: (514) 844-2001
Fax: (514) 844-6001
http://www.enroutemag.com/

Event

P.O. Box 2503
New Westminster, BC V3L 5B2
Tel: (604) 527-5293
Fax: (604) 527-5095
E-mail: event@douglas.bc.ca
http://event.douglas.bc.ca/

Exile

Exile/Excelsior Publishing Inc.
134 Eastbourne Ave.
Toronto, ON M5P 2G6
http://www.exilequarterly.com/quarterly/

The Fiddlehead

Campus House, 11 Garland Court
University of New Brunswick
P.O. Box 4400
Fredericton, NB E3B 5A3
Tel: (506) 453-3501
Fax: (506) 453-5069
E-mail: fiddlehd@unb.ca
http://www.lib.unb.ca/Texts/Fiddlehead/

Filling Station

P.O. Box 22135, Bankers Hall
Calgary, AB T2P 4J5
http://www.fillingstation.ca/

Grain Magazine

P.O. Box 67
Saskatoon, SK S7K 3K1
Tel: (306) 244-2828
Fax: (306) 244-0255
E-mail: grainmag@sasktel.net
   (queries only)
http://www.grainmagazine.ca/

Hammered Out

E-mail: hammeredout@cogeco.ca
http://hammeredoutlitzine.blogspot.com

Kiss Machine

http://www.kissmachine.org/

Lichen

http://www.lichenjournal.ca/

Literary Review of Canada

P.O. Box 8, Stn. K
Toronto, ON M4P 2G1
E-mail: poetry@lrcreview.com
http://lrc.reviewcanada.ca/

Maisonneuve Magazine

4413 Harvard Ave.
Montreal, QC H4A 2W9
Tel: (514) 482-5089
http://www.maisonneuve.org/

The Malahat Review

University of Victoria
P.O. Box 1700, Station CSC
Victoria, BC v8w 2Y2
Tel: (250) 721-8524
Fax: (250) 472-5051
E-mail: malahat@uvic.ca
http://malahatreview.ca

Matrix Magazine

1400 de Maisonneuve W., Ste. LB-658
Montreal, QC H3G 1M8
E-mail: info@matrixmagazine.org
http://www.matrixmagazine.org/

The New Quarterly

St. Jerome's University
290 Westmount Rd. N.
Waterloo, ON N2L 3G3
http://www.tnq.ca/

Prairie Fire

Prairie Fire Press, Inc.
423–100 Arthur St.
Winnipeg, MB R3B 1H3
Tel: (204) 943-9066
Fax: (204) 942-1555
E-mail: prfire@mts.net
http://www.prairiefire.ca/about.html

PRECIPICe

Department of English Language and
Literature
Brock University
500 Glenridge Ave.
St. Catharines, ON L2S 3A1
http://www.brocku.ca/precipice/

PRISM International

Creative Writing Program
University of British Columbia
Buch. E462 – 1866 Main Mall
Vancouver, BC v6T 1Z1
Tel: (604) 822-2514
Fax: (604) 822-3616
http://prism.arts.ubc.ca/

QWERTY

c/o English Department
University of New Brunswick
P.O. Box 4400
Fredericton, NB E3B 5A3
E-mail: qwerty@unb.ca
http://www.lib.unb.ca/Texts/QWERTY/

Room

P.O. Box 46160, Stn. D
Vancouver, BC v6J 5G5
http://www.roommagazine.com/

Taddle Creek

P.O. Box 611, Stn. P
Toronto, ON M5S 2Y4
E-mail: editor@taddlecreekmag.com
http://www.taddlecreekmag.com/

THIS Magazine

401 Richmond St. W., Ste. 396
Toronto, ON M5V 3A8
Editorial Tel: (416) 979-8400
Business Tel: (416) 979-9429
Fax: (416) 979-1143
E-mail: info@thismagazine.ca
http://www.thismagazine.ca/

Vallum

P.O. Box 326, Westmount Stn.
Montreal, QC H3Z 2T5
Tel/Fax: (514) 237-8946
http://www.vallummag.com/

The Walrus

19 Duncan St., Ste. 101
Toronto, ON M5H 3H1
Fax: (416) 971-8768
http://www.walrusmagazine.com/

West Coast Line

2027 East Annex
8888 University Drive
Simon Fraser University
Burnaby, BC V5A 1S6
Tel: (604) 291-4287
Fax: (604) 291-4622
E-mail: wcl@sfu.ca
http://www.westcoastline.ca/

PERMISSION ACKNOWLEDGMENTS

Tightrope Books gratefully acknowledges the authors and publishers for permission to reprint the following copyrighted works:

"The Reflecting Pool" originally appeared in PRISM International (45:3) copyright © 2007 by Maleea Acker. Used with permission of the author. "The Reflecting Pool" will also be published in Maleea Acker's forthcoming collection, *The Reflecting Pool*, (Pedlar Press, 2009).

"Americans" originally appeared in *Brick* (Summer 2007) copyright © 2007 by James Arthur. Used with permission of the author.

"To the Lighthouse" originally appeared in *Contemporary Verse 2* (30:2) copyright © 2007 by Leanne Averbach. Used with permission of the author.

"Hag-Ridden" from *Listening: The Last Poems of Margaret Avison* by Margaret Avison copyright © 2009. Published by McClelland & Stewart Ltd. Used with permission of the publisher. "Hag Ridden" originally appeared in PRISM International (46:1).

"Hunter Deary and Hospital Wing" originally appeared in *Matrix* (77) copyright © 2007 by Ken Babstock. Used with permission of the author.

"Weather" originally appeared in *Contemporary Verse 2* (30: 1) copyright © 2007 by John Wall Barger. Used with permission of the author.

"Dear Georgie" was originally published in *The Watchmaker's Table* copyright © 2008 by Brian Bartlett. Reprinted by permission of Goose Lane Editions. "Dear Georgie" first appeared in *Malahat Review* (158).

"One Bedroom Apartment" originally appeared in *Event* (36:2) copyright © 2007 by John Barton. Used with permission of the author.

"The Roll Call to the Ark" originally appeared in *Descant* (136) copyright © 2007 by Yvonne Blomer. Used with permission of the author.

"The Book Collector" from *The Book Collector and Other Poems* copyright © 2008 by Tim Bowling. Published by Nightwood Editions. Reprinted by permission of the publisher. "The Book Collector" originally appeared in *Fiddlehead* (231).

"One of us is in a Mohawk Cemetery" originally appeared in PRISM International (45:4) copyright © 2007 by Heather Cadbsy. Used with permission of the author.

"Stars, Sunday Dawn" originally appeared in *Malahat Review* (161) copyright © 2007 by Anne Compton. Used with permission of the author.

"Last One on the Moon" from *Revolver* by Kevin Connolly copyright © 2008. Published by House of Anansi. Reprinted with permission of the publisher. "Last One on the Moon" originally appeared in *Maisonneuve* (25).

"A Walker in the City" originally appeared in *En Route* (May 2007) copyright © 2007 by Méira Cook. Used with permission of the author.

"Union Station" originally appeared in *THIS Magazine*. (November/December 2007) copyright © 2007 by Dani Couture. Used with permission of the author. "Union Station" will also be published in Dani Couture's forthcoming collection, *The Handbook* (Pedlar Press).

"There, there" originally appeared in *Malahat Review* (161) copyright © 2007 by Sadiqa De Meijer. Used with permission of the author.

"Blindness" originally appeared in *Contemporary Verse 2* (30:1) copyright © 2007 by Barry Dempster. Used with permission of the author.

"The Gift" from *Crabwise to the Hounds* (Coach House Books, 2008) copyright © 2008 by Jeramy Dodds. Reprinted by permission of the publisher. "The Gift" originally appeared in *Arc* (59).

"Museum" originally appeared in *The Antigonish Review* (151) copyright © 2007 by Jeffery Donaldson. Used with permission of the author.

"Box" originally appeared in *Arc* (59) copyright © 2007 by Susan Elmslie. Used with permission of the author.

"Spineless Sonnet" originally appeared in *Maisonneuve* (25) copyright © 2007 by Jason Guriel. Used with permission of the author.

"Song of the Taxidermist" originally appeared in *Malahat Review* (159) copyright © 2007 by Aurian Haller. Used with permission of the author.

"Lost Forest" originally appeared in *Exile* (30: 4) copyright © 2007 by Jason Heroux. Used with permission of the author.

"A Digression on Hunting" originally appeared in *Fiddlehead* (231) copyright © 2007 by Iain Higgins. Used with permission of the author.

"Late Light" originally appeared in *Canadian Literature* (193) as "Late Night," copyright © 2007 by Bill Howell. Used with permission of the author.

"Auden's House" originally appeared in *Malahat Review* (159) copyright © 2007 by Helen Humphreys. Used with permission of the author.

"If it was the sea we heard (Penelope's Song)" from *The Bindery*, NeWest Press, spring 2007, copyright © 2007 by Shane Rhodes. Reprinted with permission of the publisher. "If it was the sea we heard" originally appeared in *Canadian Literature* (192).

"On King George's Crowning" originally appeared in *The Capilano Review* (3:3) copyright © 2007 by Joy Russell. Used with permission of the author.

"I Don't Remember Telling the Stepsons" originally appeared in *PRISM International* (45:2) copyright © 2007 by Heather Sellers. Used with permission of the author.

"Song for the Richardson's Ground Squirrel Whose Call is a Song for the Cry of the Short-Eared Owlet (They May One Day Meet for Dinner)" originally appeared in *Malahat Review* (158) copyright © 2007 by David Seymour. Used with permission of the author.

"Sweetness" originally appeared in *Fiddlehead* (231) copyright © 2007 by J. Mark Smith. Used with permission of the author.

"Jeremiah Scrounges Rest" originally appeared in *Fiddlehead* (231) copyright © 2007 by Adam Sol. Used with permission of the author.

"Squash Rackets" originally appeared in *Fiddlehead* (231) copyright © 2007 by Carmine Starnino. "Squash Rackets" will also be published in Carmine Starnino's forthcoming collection, *This Way Out*, (Gaspereau Press, Spring 2009).

"Morning after" originally appeared in *Room.* (30.2) copyright © 2007 by Anna Swanson. Used with permission of the author.

"Gentlemen of Nerve" originally appeared in *Vallum* (4:2-5:1) copyright © 2007 by Todd Swift. Used with permission of the author.

"Encyclopedia of Grass" originally appeared in *Fiddlehead* (231) copyright © 2007 by J.R. Toriseva. Used with permission of the author.

"Shrove Tuesday" originally appeared in *Fiddlehead* (233) copyright © 2007 by Leif E. Vaage. Used with permission of the author.

ACKNOWLEDGMENTS

PUBLISHER'S ACKNOWLEDGMENTS

Tightrope Books would like to thank David Lehman, Debby de Groot of Meisner, de Groot and Associates, Marilyn Biderman of McClelland & Stewart, and Kevin Hanson of Simon & Schuster, Canada, as well as all the publishers who graciously allowed us to use poems from their authors' collections and were patient with us in terms of rights and permissions.

Another special thank you to all the literary journals and magazines that kindly gave us subscriptions for the guest editor to draw from for *The Best Canadian Poetry in English 2008*. Thank you to Mara Korkola for the use of her art for the cover, and to Carleton Wilson of Carleton Wilson Graphic Design, without whom this book could not have been a reality. Finally, a big thank you for all your work to our fabulous inaugural Guest Editor Stephanie Bolster, our Series Editor, Molly Peacock and Managing Editor Heather Wood.

EDITOR'S ACKNOWLEDGMENTS

To the poets whose work appears here and on the list, thank you. To the editors of the journals, who generously provided copies and without whose (usually tireless and often voluntary) work this anthology would have no content, thank you. And to Halli Villegas, Molly Peacock, and everyone at Tightrope Books, for having confidence in me, thank you.

Stephanie Bolster

STEPHANIE BOLSTER's first book, *White Stone: The Alice Poems* (Signal/Véhicule), won the Governor General's Award and the Gerald Lampert Award in 1998 and appeared in French with Les Éditions du Noroît in autumn 2007, translated by Daniel Canty. She has also published *Two Bowls of Milk* (McClelland & Stewart), which won the Archibald Lampman Award and was shortlisted for the Trillium Award, and *Pavilion* (McClelland & Stewart). Her work has appeared in literary journals internationally and has also garnered her the Bronwen Wallace Award, the Norma Epstein Award, and *The Malahat Review*'s Long Poem Prize. Her several chapbooks include, most recently, *Biodôme* (above/ground) and *Past the Roman Arena and the Cedar of Lebanon* (Delirium). She is the editor of *The Ishtar Gate: Last and Selected Poems* (McGill-Queen's) by the late Ottawa poet Diana Brebner and is a co-editor of *Penned: Animals in Zoos in Poems* (Véhicule, forthcoming). Raised in Burnaby, B.C., she now lives in Montréal, where she teaches in the creative writing programme at Concordia University.

MOLLY PEACOCK is the author of five volumes of poetry, including *Cornucopia: New & Selected Poems*, published by Penguin Canada, and by W.W. Norton in the US and UK. She is the Poetry Editor of the Literary Review of Canada. Before she emigrated to Canada in 1992, she was one of the creators of Poetry in Motion on the Buses and Subways in New York City, and she served as an early advisor to Poetry On The Way. Peacock is also the author of a memoir, *Paradise, Piece by Piece*, published by McClelland and Stewart, and of a book about poetry, *How To Read A Poem & Start A Poetry Circle*, also published by M & S. Her reviews and essays have appeared in the Globe and Mail. Her poems have appeared in *The New Yorker, The Paris Review,* and the *TLS*. Recently she toured with her one-woman show in poems, "The Shimmering Verge" produced by the London, Ontario based company, Femme Fatale Productions. She lives in Toronto with her husband, Michael Groden, an English Professor at the University of Western Ontario. Her website is: www.mollypeacock.org.